THE TUNISIAN CROCHET SWEATER COLLECTION

Great Styles for Every Shape

DORA OHRENSTEIN

STACKPOLE BOOKS

Essex, Connecticut

STACKPOLE BOOKS

An imprint of The Globe Pequot Publishing Group, Inc.
64 South Main Street
Essex, CT 06426
www.globepequot.com

Copyright © 2025 Dora Ohrenstein
Photography by Scott Jones except the photos on pages 50 (top left), 104, 125, and 126

All rights reserved. No part of this book may be reproduced in any form or by any electronic or mechanical means, including information storage and retrieval systems, without written permission from the publisher, except by a reviewer who may quote passages in a review.

The contents of this book are for personal use only. Patterns herein may be reproduced in limited quantities for such use. Any large-scale commercial reproduction is prohibited without the written consent of the publisher.

We have made every effort to ensure the accuracy and completeness of these instructions. We cannot, however, be responsible for human error, typographical mistakes, or variations in individual work.

British Library Cataloguing in Publication Information available

Library of Congress Cataloging-in-Publication Data available

ISBN 978-0-8117-7656-1 (paper : alk. paper)
ISBN 978-0-8117-7657-8 (electronic)

♾™ The paper used in this publication meets the minimum requirements of American National Standard for Information Sciences—Permanence of Paper for Printed Library Materials, ANSI/NISO Z39.48-1992.

First Edition

Contents

Introduction	v
Abbreviations	vii

1 | Tunisian Crochet Essentials   1

What Is Tunisian Crochet?	1
A Hybrid Craft	2
Stitches in this Book	3
Basic Stitches, Terminology, Instructions	5
Basic Foundation Row	5
Increasing and Decreasing	7
More Technical Matters	8
Working the Last Row	8
Connecting Stitches	8
Choosing Yarns	9
Getting Gauge	10
Tools	11

2 | Sweater Fit and Construction   13

Choosing Your Size	13
Ease	13
Understanding Schematics	14
Sweater Constructions	15
Dropped Shoulder	15
Raglan	18
Other Top-Down Options	21
Finishing	21
Edgings	21
Seams	22
Button Bands and Buttons	24
Blocking	24
Where Should I Begin?	25

iii

3 | Patterns 27

Nola 28

Mimi 33

Aimee 38

Nina 45

Tina 55

Gilliam 61

Becca 67

Layla 74

Joni 79

Kelcy 86

Vanessa 93

Tess 100

Regina 105

Frida 113

Zoey 119

Acknowledgments 127
About the Author 128

Introduction

I started my crochet journey around twenty years ago, at a time when there were far fewer books to use as resources, and no videos at all. My passion was to create crochet garments, and, to learn how, I bought many used books online. One was a booklet by Bernat yarns dated 1967, with page after page of super chic fashions—not only sweaters but jackets, suits, and evening dresses—all made with Tunisian crochet. When I saw that, I knew I wanted to study Tunisian along with regular crochet. I adore both crafts but soon realized that Tunisian can yield excellent drape with heavier-weight yarns as well as a closed fabric that makes garments practical. As a designer of some two hundred or so patterns for magazines and books, I've always made Tunisian crochet a significant part of what I design.

Lovely drape and closed fabric are what make Tunisian great for garments and make those garments so wearable in everyday life. In designing the sweaters in this book, I thought a lot about this quality of wearability. Why? Because it's awesome to make sweaters that you actually feel great about wearing in public, whether dressing for work, an outing, a party, or whatever! My purpose is to give you garments you can wear with jeans or skirts, heels or sneakers, that will look fabulous in many settings and be comfortable to wear. There are items for all kinds of temperatures, too—warm winter garments like Regina and summer wear such as Tina.

What makes a garment something you love wearing? I believe it is good fit and comfort, combined with that ineffable quality we call style. When we think about contemporary fashion, there are always new and evolving trends—whether garments are slim or oversized, short or long, colorful or neutral. But each of us has a personal fashion style too. My own, reflected in these designs, is for garments that can work with many other pieces in your wardrobe, classic items that can easily be adapted to whatever trend is happening at the moment.

For a garment to look and feel this good, we do need to master a few skills beyond basic crochet. None of them is inherently difficult; each simply takes practice and time. Swatching, measuring, gauge-matching, shaping, seaming, counting stitches, and pattern reading are all skills that build as you do them, helping you gain comfort and confidence. Improved mastery will make your crochet so much more rewarding, especially when you see gorgeous fabric flowing from your hook.

There is no reason that your very first sweater can't come out well and be something you can wear proudly. But it's also true that your tenth sweater will be even more impressive! There are so many angles to sweater making, from choosing the yarn, maintaining steady gauge, and being confident in your execution of instructions to knowing what looks and fits best on your body. For those of you tackling garments for the first time, rather than be daunted, look at this as the beginning of an exciting journey. Avoid using the fanciest yarn for your first effort. Many of my designs are tried out first on my stash yarns before they are ever published. You might consider your first sweater effort more of a draft than a final version—that will take the pressure off.

    Now, some important tips to help you achieve good results: First of all, read all the introductory material on the sweater style you're making. Be organized. Be sure you have all the supplies needed. Read the pattern thoroughly, and make sure you understand everything that happens in it. Refer to earlier sections of the book for a refresher on techniques and concepts. Choose yarn wisely. Practice the stitch first, and make sure that the pattern's gauge works with your yarn. On the matter of gauge, think not only about whether you can get gauge but also about whether you can maintain it easily. Most importantly, consider whether this gauge looks good with your yarn. This will require swatching and blocking.

    Some people say they dislike swatching, or they find it a waste of time and yarn. But there is only one way to know how a stitch will look at a particular gauge with a particular yarn, and that is by working it up and blocking it (except in the few cases where fibers don't need blocking—more on that later). Once created, swatches are a valuable tool for the crafter who will, no doubt, want to use certain yarns, fibers, stitches, and techniques again. Far from being wasteful, swatches become our library of stitches worked in a variety of yarns, which in turn gives us useful information for planning future projects. The bottom line is, you are unlikely to achieve correct gauge on a project without swatching and blocking first. It's imperative if you care about fit.

    Pick your size wisely and carefully, knowing your own body measurements. Follow instructions very carefully. Count stitches every row. Work in good light. Examine your fabric often to detect any errors or flaws before it's too late. When you find errors of more than a few stitches, fix them before continuing. Check that you are maintaining gauge. Try on the garment as you go. It's easiest to do on top-down pieces, but it works with any construction. When you're working bottom up, draw the fabric around your body where it's going to be, stand in front of a mirror, and see if you have the coverage you need.

    Finishing, which includes seams as well as edgings on necklines, hems, and sleeves, is a hugely important part of the sweater. Done poorly or well, it can make or break your sweater, so plan to give it the time and attention it needs. If you're adding buttons, buy something lovely that brings out the best in the sweater but doesn't overpower it.

    If you're brand new to sweater making, begin with Nola, Mimi, or Joni. Aimee is easy, other than keeping track of colors, and would also look quite lovely in a single color if you want a more beginner-friendly version. Each pattern has its challenges. But before you begin any project from this book, I urge you to read the introductory pages that follow here, which will arm you with many tools to assist you in your sweater journey.

Abbreviations

beg	begin/beginning		**Rtn**	return pass
BL	back loop		**sc**	single crochet
ch	chain		**sc3tog**	single crochet 3 together
cm	centimeters		**Sinc**	side increase
cont	continue		**sk**	skip
dc	double crochet		**sl st**	slip stitch
dc2tog	double crochet 2 together		**sp**	space
Dec	decrease/decreasing		**st(s)**	stitch(es)
Fwd	forward pass		**Tdc**	Tunisian double crochet
g	grams		**Tdc2tog**	Tunisian double crochet 2 together
in.	inch(es)		**Tfs**	Tunisian full stitch
Inc	increase		**Tks**	Tunisian knit stitch
M	marker		**Tks2tog**	Tunisian knit stitch 2 together
m	meters		**Tps**	Tunisian purl stitch
mm	millimeters		**Tsl purled**	Tunisian slip stitch purled
oz.	ounce(s)		**Tsl st**	Tunisian slip stitch
patt	pattern		**Tss**	Tunisian simple stitch
PM	place marker		**Tss2tog**	Tunisian simple stitch 2 together
prev	previous		**WS**	wrong side
rem	remain/remaining		**X or X-st**	X-stitch
rep(s)	repeat(s)		**yd.**	yard(s)
RS	right side		**yo**	yarn over

1 | Tunisian Crochet Essentials

WHAT IS TUNISIAN CROCHET?

Curious minds may wonder about the origins of Tunisian crochet and whether it is related to the North African land of Tunisia. Before going directly to that question, let's look at the "yarn arts" in a broader context.

Among textile scholars today, it is widely accepted that knitting dates back to medieval Egypt, and specimens of early knitting exist in various museums around the world. Naturally objects of such age and fragility are damaged and incomplete, but textile study has progressed to the point that many textiles can clearly be identified as knitting or an earlier precursor to knitting called nalbinding.

But what about crochet? Has any ancient crochet been found? The answer is . . . no! While it is known that people used hooked tools to make socks and mittens in many places around the world (especially in cold climates), the concept of crochet as we know it today did not exist until the late eighteenth century. These earlier items were made with tools fashioned from home items like spoons, and they used slip stitches, which makers thought of as a form of knitting.

Beginning in the nineteenth century, textile scholarship becomes far easier due to the proliferation of printed books, pamphlets, ladies magazines, and the like, all instigated by growing economies and literacy across the world. The first crochet patterns appear in Britain in the 1840s, and the patterns are rather primitive. What's astonishing about crochet's history is how quickly it evolved from there. Gifted needlewomen—and there were many—created a vocabulary of stitches and techniques so rapidly that within the next two decades, most of the stitches we know and love today can be found in patterns from the mid-nineteenth century.

Tools, obviously, are an important part of this history. Knitting needles with a hook on one end were actually common in many parts of Europe and the Middle East, as the hook at the end was useful to knitters in all sorts of ways. The same gifted stitchers who were inventing crochet in the 1840s began to explore what could be done with this hooked knitting needle. In the mid-1850s, only ten years after the first regular crochet patterns, a brand new stitch, midway between knitting and crochet, was brought into the world. That is when Tunisian crochet first appeared.

It was not called that at first. The first pattern introduced the craft with just one stitch, called the Prince William Stitch after the new spouse of a royal princess. It was what we now call Tunisian simple stitch. In other nineteenth-century publications, it was called tricot crochet, long-hook crochet, shepherd's knitting, afghan crochet, and—get this—idiot stitch, possibly because of how simple it was. The new stitch, whatever its name, was wildly popular, and business-minded needlewomen quickly added a great variety of stitches to feed the demand. In fact, interest in Tunisian crochet persisted until the 1950s. One can find great Tunisian patterns in needlecraft publications right up to then. After that, it seems to have gone underground, for reasons I'd love to understand better.

Now, to consider the question of Tunisia: People often imagine that there exists a great book that records the names of all stitches since they first became known. But that is far from the case. These names were, in reality, developed in a haphazard way. Especially with a relatively young craft like crochet, there were no established names for stitches and techniques whatsoever. Whoever published a pattern or book was free to call things by any name they liked, and they did. But one might wonder, why would a stitch be called Tunisian?

Northern Africa in the nineteenth century was a multicultural society where many needle arts were practiced; it was also a very traditional society where crafts were passed down through generations, often without the use of books. Knitting was certainly done, and possibly regular crochet during this period as well. But no evidence, whether in the form of historic textiles or printed matter, has shown up anywhere to indicate that what we now call Tunisian crochet was practiced in Tunisia at that time.

The truth about names for crafts is that they are often invented for the purpose of marketing by writers, magazine editors, and, in fact, everyone involved in selling and distributing information about the craft to the public. When this new stitch appeared, a name suggesting an exotic but little-known (to most Europeans) location was just the thing to appeal to needle enthusiasts looking for something exciting and different. By the twentieth century, the name "Tunisian crochet" seems to have won out over other names, although afghan stitch was commonly used too.

What's particularly interesting about this craft is that, unlike regular crochet, which is so well developed and documented, Tunisian still offers a lot to explore and discover. Tunisian crochet today attracts both knitters and crocheters, and, in this fertile ground, new stitches and techniques are being invented by creative "yarnies." Twenty-first-century Tunisian crochet is bringing excitement and a sense of discovery to the needle arts. It's a stimulating moment in textile history that we celebrate in this book.

A HYBRID CRAFT

Tunisian is legitimately called a hybrid of knitting and crochet. It is both like and unlike each of these other crafts. It is like knitting in that we place a series of loops—what are called "live stitches"—on the needle. For knitters, once all the loops are on the needle, they have completed a row of work. As the next row is worked, the live stitches are transferred onto the second needle. But in Tunisian crochet, there is only one tool, a Tunisian hook, rather than two knitting needles. For that reason, we work the live stitches off the needle—now a shaft attached to a hook—by executing two "passes" for each row of work. There is a forward pass, where we place loops on the shaft, and then a return pass, where we work them off one loop at a time. **The return pass creates a row of chains that sits between the strands of the forward pass.**

Tunisian stitches may look like knitting, but because of the two passes, the fabric is thicker than typical knitted fabric. This, in turn, means we must use a considerably larger tool than a knitter would for the same weight of fabric; otherwise the fabric will be too dense and heavy. The end effect, naturally, is that Tunisian stitches are much larger than knitted ones. Garments can go a lot quicker with Tunisian crochet than they do with knitting, and they will be thicker and warmer. Please don't think that Tunisian fabric need be stiff, however.

It's important to find a hook size and stitch that will afford the drapey fabric we desire in garments.

Tunisian crochet is like regular crochet in that we use a single-hooked tool, but it needs to have a longer shaft than a regular crochet hook in order to collect live loops on the forward pass. In regular crochet every stitch is finished as it's made, and at the end of the work we simply turn and work in the other direction. Tunisian can only be worked in one direction unless using a double-ended hook and two balls of yarn. This results in fabric that looks quite different on the right and wrong sides, and for this reason Tunisian fabric is not reversible.

In regular crochet we make significant use of stitches of various heights, from compact little single crochet stitches to doubles, trebles, double trebles, and so on. Many of the lovely stitch patterns for regular crochet exploit the use of these taller and shorter stitches, and this is, in fact, a very significant feature of how crochet has been used, whether for doilies and other fine lace, motifs worked in the round, or elaborate colorwork.

One can use taller stitches in Tunisian crochet as well, but they tend to create gaps in the fabric that aren't always welcome or practical. Therefore, most Tunisian stitch patterns are based on shorter stitches, similar to single crochet. These short stitches can be executed in a great variety of ways, depending on where we insert the hook as we pick up loops on the forward pass. By inserting our hook in one way or another, we create Tunisian simple stitch, Tunisian knit stitch, Tunisian purl stitch, and an abundance of combinations of them, yielding striking visual effects. In this way, Tunisian crochet is more like knitting and can resemble knitted fabric more than crochet fabric can.

Because of the potential for density in Tunisian crochet, when we switch from regular to Tunisian crochet we must remember to increase the hook size. So, for example, if I typically use an E or F hook when working with sock weight yarn, in Tunisian I will choose a size H or I. People often use the rule of thumb "go up two sizes," but I think it can be quite a bit more. It all depends on the stitch you are using, as they have very different degrees of density and drape.

The evolution of Tunisian crochet has quite recently given us a new tool—the cabled Tunisian hook—that significantly extends what we can do with this craft. The long, flexible shaft allows us to load enough loops on for a garment, and the suppleness of a cable serves our purpose better on a curved neckline than a solid shaft of metal or bamboo.

STITCHES IN THIS BOOK

Many stitch patterns have been developed in Tunisian, and I've chosen some of the most popular. There are sweaters made with Tunisian simple stitch, Tunisian knit stitch, and Tunisian honeycomb stitch, all of which are familiar to most crafters who've tried Tunisian crochet. Then there are sweaters made with somewhat less common stitches, both for solid, closed fabric and for something a bit more open. My aim is to offer a variety of fabrics suitable for different seasons and to give crafters something new they haven't encountered before. But none of the stitches is difficult to execute after a little practice.

For each stitch in the book, a gauge swatch can be used not only to measure gauge but to get comfortable with the stitch before you go on to the full sweater. The gauge swatches can be made fairly small, but for mastering the stitch, I urge you to do much larger swatches. Nothing educates a crafter like swatching and carefully examining how your stitches look. It teaches you how to manage tension, so that stitches are clear and even, and to create fabric that is supple. Furthermore, a larger swatch will give you a much more accurate reading of your actual gauge and of whether it matches the pattern's.

Tunisian crochet should always be worked with a loose hand. Forward pass stitches that are pulled too tight will look cramped, so when drawing up loops, give them some breathing room around the shaft and avoid any tightening of the stitch, once made. The return row is nothing more than a series of chain stitches, and you want nice, loose chains that will sit between the loops of the forward pass, spanning from one stitch to the next without clumping them together. In all but the Tunisian knit stitch, the return row is visible and should have that same relaxed look and feel as the forward pass.

It can take a while to adjust to working loosely, partly because of the appearance of your work. The row you are working on looks far looser than it will be once the following row is worked into it. The big loops on your hook will be filled in with return row stitches, and the forward row loops will lift and tighten those loops further. This is why practicing on a swatch is so helpful and important.

The basic stitches you will need to know to make these patterns are: Tunisian simple stitch (Tss), Tunisian purl stitch (Tps), Tunisian full stitch (Tfs), and Tunisian double crochet (Tdc). Yes, we do use one taller stitch in several stitch patterns, and it adds fabulous texture, as you'll see. If any of these are new to you, learn and practice them so you're really comfortable before going further.

Another technique used in some stitch patterns involves working a different kind of return row. Whereas the basic stitches use a basic return pass, always pulling one chain through one loop on the hook, some of our stitches require pulling one return row chain through several loops on the hook. That's how the little upside-down fans are created in photos at right. When working these stitches, in order to maintain the correct stitch counts, we also have to add chains on that return pass.

You'll encounter these stitch patterns:

Tunisian Simple Stitch in Gilliam

Tunisian Knit Stitch in Nola

Tunisian Honeycomb Stitch, consisting of Tss and Tps, from Joni and Mimi

Tunisian Rib Stitch, consisting of Tks and Tps, from Kelcy

Tunisian X stitch with Tps, from Vanessa

Tunisian shells with Tss in Becca and Aimee

Tunisian Puff Stitches with Tps in Zoey

Tunisian double crochet stitches with Tps in Layla

Tunisian knit stitch with yarnovers in Nina

Tunisian simple stitch with Tunisian slip stitch purled in Tina

BASIC STITCHES, TERMINOLOGY, INSTRUCTIONS

Most Tunisian crochet begins with a basic foundation row. You chain a certain number, and for the first forward pass, you draw up a loop in each chain. When doing this, it's your choice whether to insert the hook in the back loop of each chain or in the back bump. Some folks have strong preferences for one or the other. I like to use the first method simply because it's faster. Use whichever you prefer for any of the designs in this book. In any case, once you have all the forward loops made, you begin the return pass.

Basic Foundation Row

Instructions for the basic foundation row are:
Fwd: Draw up a loop in each ch. **Rtn:** Yo, draw through 1 loop, *yo, draw through 2 loops, rep from * across.

When you've completed these two passes, you will have the same number of Tunisian stitches as the number of chains with which you began.

Note that the beginning of the return pass—"yo, draw through 1 loop"—is equivalent to making a chain 1. When you have completed the return pass, you will have 1 loop on your hook, and it becomes the first stitch of the following forward pass. **Therefore, every forward pass begins with the first stitch already on your hook, and the next stitch you make is worked into the second stitch of the row below.** It's similar to how the turning chain works in regular crochet; but in Tunisian, the first stitch is already made and sitting on your hook.

The result of having this loop on the hook when you begin a row is that the starting edge is not in pattern. That's fine, as it gives the edge a nice finish. But what about the opposite edge, at the ends of rows? Here the standard technique is to insert the hook as if you are making a Tunisian knit stitch—between the front and back vertical bars of the stitch. Done at the end of a row, it doesn't look like Tks but matches the opposite edge nicely and creates a firm edge. This is called "end stitch" in instructions.

Most of the patterns in this book begin with a basic foundation row; instructions will simply say "work basic foundation row." "Work basic return row" will be used where only the forward pass needs to be spelled out. At times a return pass will be referred to as a return row. Please don't let it throw you. In common parlance, the term "pass" is rarely used. It is used here and in other technical books to make clear that a complete Tunisian row has two parts. But in everyday talk about Tunisian, we often speak of a forward row and a return row and therefore you will also find those terms used in these pages.

One more important point to make about the foundation row: Although it resembles Tss, that is

Tunisian Crochet Essentials

an illusion! The stitch really only becomes whatever it is when we work the next forward pass. This can be hard to visualize, but once you're actually doing Tunisian crochet, it's very clear. **Stitches are always defined by how we work into them in the following row.**

Here are a few more terms we use in Tunisian crochet. The loops on the forward pass all have a **front and back vertical bar**. We use the term "vertical bar" to differentiate these loops from the return pass, which runs in a horizontal direction. Different stitches are made by inserting the hook in different ways in relation to these vertical bars as we draw up loops to make stitches.

Drawing up a loop is a pretty simple maneuver. You may have come across Tunisian instructions where this is written: "Yo, pull through." Language for Tunisian is not completely standardized, and I find it simpler to say "Draw up a loop," so that's what you'll find throughout this book.

For example, for Tunisian simple stitch, we insert the hook into the front vertical bar and draw up a loop.

For Tunisian knit stitch, we insert the hook between the front and back vertical bars and draw up a loop.

For Tunisian full stitch (Tfs), we insert the hook between adjacent vertical bars and draw up a loop.

For the stitches described thus far, the working yarn is behind the work, as it normally is in crochet. Tunisian purl stitch (Tps) is created by bringing the working yarn to the front of the work, then inserting into the next vertical bar and drawing up a loop.

Tunisian double crochet (Tdc) is similar to what's done in regular crochet, but not identical. Instructions will read: "Yo, insert hook in next vertical bar and draw up a loop, yo, draw through 2 loops, leaving 1 loop on hook." In regular crochet we would draw through 2 loops twice, but in Tunisian we need to have one loop on the hook. When working into the Tdc in the following row, you will see that it too has vertical bars at the top. Here are two Tunisian double crochet stitches worked into the same stitch (from our Layla design).

Here are instructions for the forward pass of basic stitches with standard abbreviations:

Tss: Insert hook in next vertical bar and draw up a loop.

Tks: Insert hook between front and back vertical bars and draw up a loop.

Tfs: Insert hook between 2 vertical bars and draw up a loop.

Tps: Bring yarn to front, insert hook in next vertical bar and draw up a loop.

All these stitches use the basic return pass we've discussed.

For the designs in this book, only Tss and Tks are used for an entire garment. Tfs, Tps, and Tdc are always combined with other stitches to create a stitch pattern. Every stitch pattern behaves a bit differently and will create a particular look on the surface and a specific kind of drape in the fabric.

With that in mind, take note that Tunisian purl stitch is a very loose stitch by nature. You may have the urge to tighten it up, but please don't. It is the contrast between Tps and other stitches used in combination with it that results in the desired look and feel of the stitch pattern.

As for Tunisian knit stitch, it really does look like knitting on the surface, but it tends to be a tight stitch. When working this stitch, we want to resist its tendency to tighten, so take extra care to work Tks loosely, especially on the forward pass.

INCREASING AND DECREASING

An interesting feature of Tunisian crochet is that the two passes give us many options when increases or decreases in stitch counts are required. This occurs in all the patterns, as sweaters need to be a certain shape to fit the body. Fabric is shaped by changing the number of stitches and/or rows, either adding more or removing them.

To increase in Tunisian crochet, we need to draw up a loop somewhere other than the next vertical bar. We can use the back vertical bar, which is written as "Insert hook in back vertical bar and draw up loop," meaning that we insert the hook behind that bar and pull yarn through. We can insert the hook in the space between stitches, which is the same as making a Tfs. We can also insert the hook into a chain of the return row, a method I use frequently in this book. Simply insert under the topmost strand of the chain and draw yarn through.

To decrease stitches on the forward pass, we insert the hook under two vertical bars and draw up a loop, thereby eliminating one of the stitches. In Tss, this is easy. In Tks, we insert the hook into the first stitch of the decrease as if making a Tss, then insert as if making a Tks, that is, between the front and back vertical bars in the second stitch of the decrease. Where the stitch pattern involves various basic stitches, we may or may not be able to pick up the two stitches in the pattern. When we can't, the same strategy is used as in Tks decreases, that is, the first stitch of the decrease is worked like a Tss, and the second stitch is worked in pattern. How to make decreases is always spelled out in instructions.

At times, I've used the return pass for decreases, as it may yield a better-looking result. This can often occur at the front neckline. In these cases, as you are working the return row, you will draw through more than the usual two loops. We've already discussed how this can be used to create different stitch patterns. When decreasing for shaping sweater necklines, this happens at the beginning or end of the return pass. What can be confusing at times is counting the loops to pull through. Our Tunisian terminology uses the word "loop" to refer to the loops on the shaft or cable in the forward row, but there is also the "working loop," the one that is on the hook.

When instructions say to work the return pass "to last 4 loops" or "until there are 4 loops on hook" (or some other number), the loops on the shaft and the one close to the hook are included in that number.

Shaping with rows is very straightforward and is associated with the length measurements of garments: body length, yoke length, or sleeve length. You can change the lengths of body and sleeve easily by working more or fewer rows, and options for this are detailed in many patterns.

You will find more on shaping in the sections on sweater construction that follow.

MORE TECHNICAL MATTERS

There are a few technical challenges in Tunisian crochet that should be mentioned. The most significant is the tendency of Tunisian fabric to curl rather than lie flat. Much of this is caused by a failure to work with a loose hand or to use the correct hook size. When loose tension is used, much of the curling is eliminated. Any remaining curl must be stamped out by blocking.

Another concern is the tendency of the first stitch in the row to enlarge, which in turn means the starting edge of the work can be longer than the ending edge. Keep the first few stitches in the forward pass a bit tighter to compensate for this tendency. Still, even for experienced Tunisian crocheters, there can be a discrepancy in the lengths of side edges. Either through blocking or other finishing strategies, this can be brought under control so that the finished garment is symmetrical.

You may encounter Tunisian stitches that cause the fabric to slant—somewhat to the right if you're right-handed and to the left if you're left-handed. Some stitches are more prone to this than others

are, and in fact, there are some I swatched for this book that were simply not usable. In instances where a stitch has this slant to it, be sure to use yarns that can be wet blocked. Just like curl, blocking can entirely remove the slant and your garment will end up neatly balanced.

WORKING THE LAST ROW

You may recall that a row of Tunisian stitches is defined by how we work into it on the following row. Well then, how do we make our last row of work match the rest of the fabric? The answer is, we continue inserting our hook in the pattern, but instead of leaving loops on the hook, we pull the working yarn through the loop on the hook. These are called Tunisian slip stitches worked in pattern. We are working the stitch and making a slip stitch at the same time. These are spelled out in instructions as Tss sl st, Tks sl st, and Tps sl st.

The exception to this is when working with Tks. I find that Tks slip stitches leave a crooked edge that curls, so I avoid it and work the last Tunisian slip stitch row using a different stitch, spelled out in each pattern, of course.

CONNECTING STITCHES

One thing that's a bit tricky in Tunisian crochet is working in the round, with the last stitch of the row connecting to the first neatly and unobtrusively. Some clever people have now popularized a technique called "connecting stitches" that makes it possible to do this. After working the last stitch of the forward pass, you insert the hook in two strands of the first stitch in the same row—the back loop of the vertical bar and also the back loop of the return row chain—then yarn over and draw through 3 loops to begin the return row, instead of just one as we normally do. It's wise to mark those 2 loops so you can easily see them.

Yellow marker placed in 2 loops in first stitch of row

Hook inserted into 2 marked loops

Connecting stitch completed

Here is an excellent page with both photos and video showing the technique: https://rachelhenri.com/en/simple-connecting-stitch/#more-2445.

CHOOSING YARNS

What are your criteria for choosing yarns for sweaters? Let me share the considerations that are foremost in my mind.

The chief quality I focus on is that of drape—the way fabric hangs and folds around the body. This can be an elusive quality in crochet, as the fabric tends to be denser than knitted fabric. Yarns can be chosen to enhance this quality. The thinner the yarn used, the more fluid the fabric. On the other hand, we don't necessarily want to work with fingering and lace weight yarns in every project. In fact, this book uses a variety of yarn weights, from fingering to sport to DK and worsted, yet all the garments have excellent drape.

Heavier weight yarns can have good drape if they are worked at a loose gauge. Stitches also affect drape in a major way. For example, Tunisian knit stitch is by nature dense, and therefore I used the most soft and flexible yarns I could find and a large hook to ensure that the Tunisian knit garments (Nola and Frida) have this desired fluidity. Tunisian purl stitch, on the other hand, is loose and enhances drape, so you will find several stitch patterns incorporating purls here (Mimi, Joni, Kelcy). Openwork stitches—not quite lace, but with some space between stitches—are used in Vanessa, Gilliam, and Becca. A mesh-type lace is featured in Nina, a garment that exemplifies drape.

Other elements that affect drape include the fibers of the yarn and how the yarn is spun and twisted. Yarn companies make yarns for different purposes, and it's wise to learn as much as you can about a yarn before investing money and effort. An afghan meant to withstand daily use and frequent machine washing is best made with a very hardy yarn. For a garment, however, we need soft, flexible fibers that feel great on the skin and will hug the body in flattering ways when worn. Some cottons have this quality, while others are stiffer and more appropriate for amigurumi. The same is true for wools. They range from soft and squishy to tough and scratchy.

Tunisian Crochet Essentials **9**

Both natural fibers as well as acrylics can be made for good drape. Natural fibers generally are more fragile and require more care, but to me, the beauty they add to a garment makes it worth the extra effort. Which takes me to the next consideration I bring to yarn: Is it pretty? Is there a sheen, an interesting texture or color? I go into more depth on how I chose each yarn in the introduction to each sweater.

We've all encountered the reality that not all yarn weights are the same across various manufacturers. One company's worsted can be another's DK! Though maddening, it's a fact of yarnie life. That's why picking your yarns wisely is so crucial. If you use a heavier weight yarn than was used in the pattern, your fabric will be markedly different: heavier and denser. If you use a lighter weight, the fabric may have unwanted gaps. Gather as much information as you can before purchasing, and don't neglect swatching, which will reveal all.

Choosing a different fiber than what the pattern calls for is not necessarily a bad thing at all, so long as you can get gauge and drape. Many of my designs could be done with an animal fiber for cold weather and a cotton, linen, or bamboo for summer.

You'll also want to take note of the structure of the yarn—that is, whether it's a single or plied yarn, loosely or tightly twisted, textured or fuzzy. Single-ply yarns give great stitch definition and look fabulous, but they are less resilient over the long haul and more apt to pill. Loosely twisted yarns will give you better drape on your garment than tightly twisted will. Heavily textured yarn will obscure individual stitches, and fuzzy yarns may look thin but act like a heavier weight than you think. Do read the label and, even better, visit the manufacturer's website. You'll find a lot of good information there. Most companies will specify when a yarn is apt for garment making. Baby yarns can be very nice for this purpose as they are meant to be soft and flexible, but they are not usually available in a range of colors.

If you are venturing into sweater making without much experience, I encourage you to sample different yarns before purchasing large quantities. You can also research on sites like ravelry.com to see what other makers are using for their wearables.

Please note that the yardage for specific yarns included in these patterns is subject to change. I recommend checking the current yardage and adjusting the number of balls needed accordingly.

GETTING GAUGE

Every hook recommendation in standard patterns is followed by the words "or size needed to obtain gauge." Since this is so important, I've replaced that language with the heading "suggested hook size," because, truly, this is something you'll have to test yourself. I tend to be on the loose side as a stitcher, but many crocheters work rather tightly. I bet you already know which kind you are. Therefore, swatch, swatch, swatch. Your yarn may be quite different than the pattern's, and your tension is likely to be different from mine too. Gauge *is* important in garment-making, and I urge you to take the necessary time to select the hook size that will get you to it.

It's not always easy, even for the most experienced crocheter, to match and maintain gauge. There are so many factors that affect it: not only the yarn, fiber, stitch, and hook but also your mood, how much sleep you got, and the like. I highly recommend checking your gauge often as you work, rather than assuming you are maintaining it consistently. Especially with the large pieces of fabric involved in (almost) seamless sweater designs, gauge can be challenging, as the weight of the fabric itself can cause gauge to enlarge.

When measuring gauge in your Tunisian swatches, be sure to include the return row. **For the purpose of measuring gauge, every Tunisian stitch consists of the vertical bar and also the return row chain that goes with it.** If you count

The Tunisian Crochet Sweater Collection

only the bars, your gauge will not be accurate. When measuring your work for gauge, place your ruler on a vertical bar and end just before a vertical bar, so that you are including the return row chain that goes with your last stitch.

Row gauge is measured in a similar manner.

Another important point about your gauge swatch is this: Do not purposely aim for the specified gauge as you work the swatch. Work in your usual way, at a tension that you can easily maintain over the span of a large piece of fabric. If you are over or under gauge, you can then reswatch with a smaller or larger hook. Maintaining gauge is so important; you don't want to force your hands to work at a tension to which they aren't accustomed.

Remember to block your swatch. Before blocking it, you should be close to gauge but can be a little under it. "A little" in this instance means a fraction of an inch. Then block it and see if it easily stretches to gauge. Block it in the same way you intend to block the finished sweater (see page 24 for more on different ways to block).

It bears repeating here that the larger you make your gauge swatch, the more accurate it will be. The gauge swatches in this book are fairly small, but I would encourage you to make them twice as large for greater accuracy. Just double the length of the starting chain of the gauge swatch and any stitch counts that follow. This is all part of the preparations that are essential before you begin making your sweater. We know how much crocheters love to "dive in" to a project, but trust me, diving into a sweater is likely to cause frustration, wasted effort, and swimming with frogs, if you get my meaning. (Note: To yarnies, frogging is pulling out your work.)

TOOLS

There are a great variety of cabled Tunisian hooks available. Since everyone has their own preferences as to metal or bamboo, rounded or pointy hooks, and so on, I encourage you to find whatever is most comfortable. Hook sizes used for the designs range from size F (3.75 mm) to size L (8 mm).

Another very simple tool used frequently here is the stitch marker. Those used for crochet are like safety pins, but they're rounded, made of plastic, and usually come in several colors. These are preferable to actual safety pins, as the latter can easily catch on yarn.

2 | Sweater Fit and Construction

CHOOSING YOUR SIZE

To make a sweater that fits, it's wise to take a few crucial measurements on your body. This will allow you to pick the right size, since measurements will appear on each sweater's schematic.

The width measurements to take on your body are the circumferences at four different points: the bust, the upper arm (or bicep), and the high and low hip. Take these measurements with a measuring tape. For bust and upper arm, put the measuring tape around the largest point on your body to be sure you know the coverage needed. The high hip is at the top of the pelvic bone and the low hip is around the buttocks. Many sweaters stop at the high hips, but some extend to the low hips.

One more width measurement that's good to know is your shoulder width. Measure from one outside edge of the collarbone to the other. You can usually find that spot by feeling the joint between your collarbone and arm, but don't worry too much about exactly where it is. Some shoulder widths can be a bit broader, others narrower, depending on the garment's style. In general, shoulder widths will range from 13 in./33 cm to 19 in./ 48 cm across all sizes.

Now take some length measurements: one from an inch below the armpit to your high hip and one from the same point to your low hip. This measurement is called the body length, and some sweaters, as previously mentioned, will extend to one or the other, while others are more cropped.

Now take another measurement from this same point—an inch below the armpit—straight up to the top of your shoulder. This measurement is called armhole depth, and it is the length of the armhole of the sweater. We always add that extra inch or two below the armhole to make sweaters comfortable and allow freedom of movement.

Another length measurement that's useful is for the sleeves. Measure along the arm, again about an inch away from the armpit, down to the wrist. Then take another measurement down to just below the elbow. This will give you good measurements for long and midlength sleeves. Some designs in this book have sleeves midway between these points. Once you have your length measurements, it will be easy for you to determine how different sleeve lengths will work on your body, and modifying lengths for sleeves will be an easy adjustment.

Write all your numbers down and keep all this information in a safe place where you can easily refer to it.

EASE

Sweaters often have extra fabric for width measurements, which is called ease. Ease can be as little as 1 in./2.5 cm over the circumference measurement, or it can be several inches over that measurement. Sometimes a sweater can look great with no ease at all, meaning it measures exactly the same as bust circumference, or with negative ease, meaning it measures a little less than actual bust. Depending on how you like a sweater to fit, you can consider anywhere from negative or no ease to 4 in./10 cm of ease over your circumference measurements on the bust and hips, and up to 2 in./5 cm on the sleeves. At the moment, oversized sweaters are in fashion, and we have some here that have much more ease—as much as 8 in./20 cm extra over bust circumference. For length measurements, we do not add any ease, except for the extra inch or two for armhole depth discussed earlier. The weight of crochet garments exerts downward pull; it adds an inch or two of ease when the garment is worn compared to the length when it is lying flat.

If you aren't sure about your preferences on some of these matters of fit, I recommend you measure your favorite sweaters. Lay them flat and measure them with a ruler. Measure the width at the bust, bicep, and hips. Of course, you'll have to double these numbers to obtain the circumferences. Take some length measurements as well, from the bottom of the sweater's armhole to its hem, from the bottom of the armhole to the top of the shoulder, and from the bottom of the armhole to the bottom of the sleeve. Write it all down somewhere to keep.

Most likely you will find a range of measurements in your sweaters, and this will give you a good idea of what sweater dimensions work best for you and how they will look on your body. Your next task is to consult the schematic for the sweater you're making and see which size suits your body best.

UNDERSTANDING SCHEMATICS

We're using sizes 1 through 5, which roughly correspond to small, medium, large, 1X, and 2X, in this book, but please don't rely on the size you choose for manufactured garments. These sizes, as we all know, can vary significantly. **What counts when choosing your size are the actual dimensions of the finished sweater as they compare to your measurements.**

Those dimensions are to be found on each sweater's schematic. A schematic is simply a drawing with lines and numbers indicating important measurements for fit. Here is a schematic for Becca.

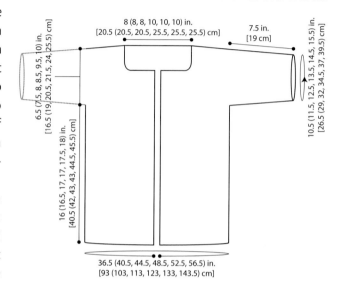

For most sweaters, the bust and hip circumferences are the same, and you will see them at the bottom of the drawing. If they are not the same, as you will see in Zoey and Regina, both measurements appear at the bottom of the drawing, the bust above the hip circumference. The sleeve circumference is indicated along the sleeve near the bicep. Some schematics include a measurement for the circumference at the bottom of the sleeve as well.

The length measurements are shown along the side, with lines and dots showing beginning and end points. The top line indicates armhole depth, the distance from the shoulder to the bottom of the armhole, and the lower one is body length, the distance from the bottom of the armhole to the bottom of the sweater.

Two more width measurements that you will see are the back neck width and the neck circumference. Both of these are intended to give

The Tunisian Crochet Sweater Collection

you a sense of how close-fitting the garment is around the neck, whether close-fitting or more open-necked. Back neck width is associated with sweaters made bottom up. These always end with two shoulder sections that have some space in between, and it's the space between that we measure for back neck width. Sweaters that are close-fitting at the neck will range from 5 in./13 cm to 8 in./20 cm of back neck width over the range of sizes. Where you see larger measurements than these, the fit is wider—for example, Gilliam. Because I want all the sweaters to be functional and not fall off the shoulders, you won't see great variation in these back neck measurements.

On the top-down sweaters, we start with the neckline, and therefore, there is no divide for the neck or shoulders. Instead, we measure the entire neckline circumference. Close-fitting necklines will range from 22 in./56 cm to 28 in./71 cm. An example of a larger neckline circumference is Zoey.

If you want to get a feel for the neckline circumference on your body, take your tape measure, make a circle with it at the neck circumference measurement indicated for your size, and put it over your head. The circle should be centered on your head, rather than pulled down in front, so that it sits the same distance at the front and back. You can easily see whether the neckline is close-fitting or more relaxed. But there's one more caveat: We calculate the number of inches based on the stitch counts for the first row of the pattern. But when worn, the neckline edges fan out, thereby naturally enlarging it by an inch or two. So, if the 22 in./56 cm neckline on Vanessa seems rather small, you can see how it works on the model, where it is not tight around the neck at all.

There are two more measurements on schematics that tell you how deep the neckline is, which we call neck depth. This is measured from the top of your shoulder close to the neck straight down the body. A close-fitting neck is generally 2–4 in./5–10 cm in depth. The halter has a deeper neck, as do the V-neck sweaters. To check these measurements on yourself, place your tape measure at the shoulder close to the neck and measure straight down to see where the bottom of the neckline will fall. Examples of deeper necklines are Gilliam and Mimi.

SWEATER CONSTRUCTIONS
Dropped Shoulder

The sweaters here are grouped together according to whether they are worked bottom up or top down. Most of the bottom-up sweaters use the simplest construction, called dropped shoulder. The name reflects the fact that there is no shaping for the armhole, so the outside edge of the sweater at the shoulders will extend beyond your shoulders and end at a point on the upper arm. This is a sporty, relaxed look that's quite popular at the moment.

Dropped-shoulder sweaters begin at the bottom of the sweater as simple large rectangles. The rectangle's width must be as large as the dimension you need for your hips and bust, both front and back, plus desired ease. In other words, the rectangle covers the entire bust and hip circumference. If it's a pullover, you'll eventually make one seam at the sweater's side or use a connecting stitch at the ends of rows. If a cardigan, the opening is at the center front, and no seam is needed. When we have enough length in the rectangle to arrive at the bottom of the armhole, we must work the front and back of the garment separately in order to create two armholes. Here are diagrams to help you visualize the process. The first shows a pullover and the second a cardigan.

The upper portion of the sweater, from the bottom of the armhole to the shoulder, is called the yoke. Each design has a Back and Front Yoke.

After finishing the Body, we count stitches to create these sections of the yoke, using stitch markers to demarcate each section. Since you are about to begin a new section, you may see an instruction to end off or to "place working loop on holder." The working loop is the one on your hook, and this simply means that you will pick up this loop again at a later point. Put a stitch marker in the loop to secure it.

Generally, we work the Back Yoke first, then the Front, as the Back is less complicated. The Front requires shaping for the neck, and this happens on the final portion of the Front Yoke. Front and Back Yokes will then be seamed together across the top of the shoulder.

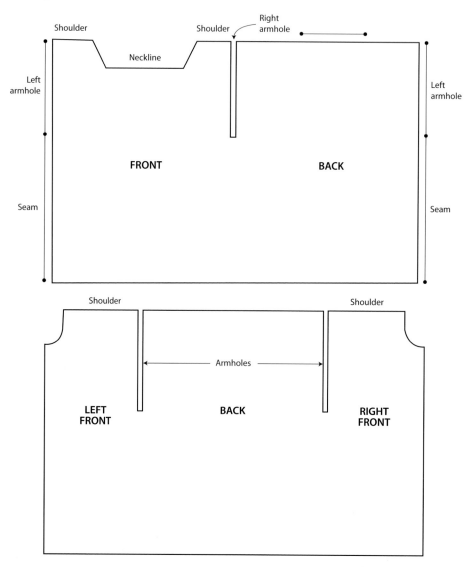

16

Some designs have shoulder shaping at the very top of the garment, to account for the natural slope of the shoulders. Only two or three rows are required, and they can make a difference on how the sweater fits.

Once the Back and Front Yokes are done, you will have a sweater with short sleeves—that extra fabric that drops over from the shoulders. Some of the designs (such as Mimi and Layla) stop there, and some have longer sleeves, which are worked by joining yarn on the existing sleeve and working down from this point to whatever sleeve length is desired. The sleeves are worked flat, with the edges meeting at the center of the underarm.

When we begin the sleeve, we join at that center point at the underarm and work around the existing sleeve, coming back to that same starting point. Sleeves are generally shaped so that they narrow as they approach the wrist. The shaping involves working decreases at regular intervals along the edges of the sleeve. When the sleeve is done, it will be seamed. Connecting stitches are impractical for sleeves, as even cabled hooks won't curve well over this smaller span.

The drawing below shows a dropped-shoulder sweater with a V-neck and a shaped sleeve.

These dropped-shoulder sweaters are easy and fun to make. But since we are not creating any shaping at the armhole, they tend to have some extra fabric that can bunch up at the underarm. Note that some of the dropped-shoulder designs here, for example, Layla and Becca, have a very close fit, which minimizes this issue.

Two designs that are worked bottom up—Nola and Tina—are not dropped-shoulder designs. Rather, they have a shaped armhole, which eliminates the extra fabric that would otherwise drop down on the arm. These designs are constructed in the same way as what's described above, up to the point of the yoke. To achieve a more fitted upper body, decreases are worked at the start of the yoke, narrowing the fabric so that the shoulders

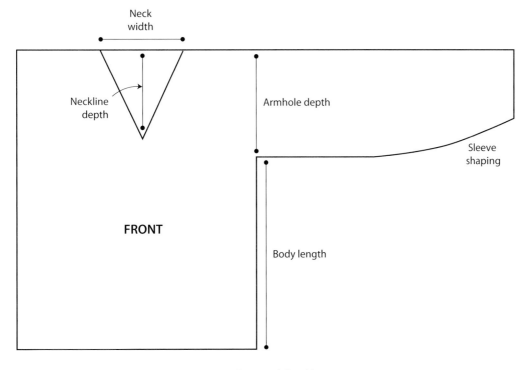

Dropped shoulder

Sweater Fit and Construction **17**

will be a few inches smaller than the bust. The dimension at the top across the shoulders is called shoulder width, a measure you've taken earlier.

Below is a schematic showing a shaped armhole, sometimes called a fitted armhole.

Another exception is Nina, an openwork jacket that is worked in vertical rows instead of the usual horizontal rows. The construction is dropped shoulder, but the direction of work is different. Instead of beginning at the bottom of the sweater, Nina begins with a row that goes from the bottom hem to the neck at the garment's center back.

We've mentioned the connecting stitch, which is a choice for any pullover in this book. When not using a connecting stitch, either for the body or a sleeve, we use the term "worked flat." There's really no major difference in the finished product, and you'll have to master either the connecting stitch itself or your seaming skills so that your finished pieces are polished and neat.

Raglan

Another construction represented here is the top-down raglan. These begin at the neckline and proceed to build a yoke by making increases at four points. The four points indicate the edges of the front and back and the two sleeves. We designate a stitch at each point as the raglan stitch, place a

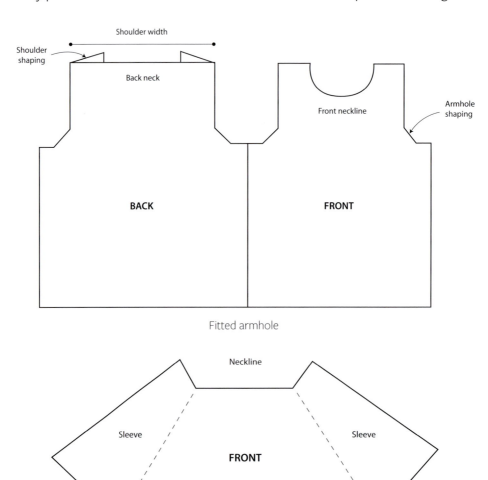

marker in it to make it easy to see, and then work an increase just before and after each marked stitch. So although there are four increase points, we are actually increasing by eight stitches. Here is a schematic of the yoke of a raglan top.

When making a raglan yoke, we generally increase on each row. But since we need to add more fabric for the sweater's front and back than for the sleeves, there will be a point where increases are not made on the sleeves, only on Front and Back. Of course, all this is spelled out for each pattern. Another variation is that some of the raglan sweaters have not one raglan stitch but three or four stitches along the raglan line. It's purely decorative and does not make the work harder; it only affects where the increases are made, and instructions detail how to place markers so you know just when to make your increase and when not to do so.

To be successful with your raglan sweaters, count stitches every row to be sure you've done all the correct increases. **Where the pattern breaks down the stitch counts for the Front, Back, and Sleeve, count your stitches between markers to be sure they match.** Note that where you see these stitch counts in a pattern, the raglan stitches are not included. You will see the total stitch count that includes all the stitches in the row and then, below that, the breakdown for stitches between markers.

Sweater Fit and Construction

Don't neglect to move your markers up every single row, because even though it may seem you can "eyeball" where to place the increase, Tunisian can be very deceptive that way. So when the pattern says to move markers up every row, I urge you to do it.

Once the raglan yoke is completed, it's time to divide the yoke up into its four components—Front, Back, and two Sleeves—so that we can join the Front to the Back and finish the Body and each Sleeve. There is one more little step to be done right at this moment, and it has to do with creating some extra fabric for the side of the body. What we do is add a few chains going from one raglan marker to the other on the garment's right and left sides. I call these underarm chains because that's exactly where they are located when the garment is worn.

When we work Row 1 of the Body, we'll draw up loops in each of those chains so that the extra fabric becomes part of the row. Those same underarm chains will be used for the Sleeves, where you will be working into the base of the underarm chains, which now have Body stitches worked into them. It's not hard to work into these base chains, but look closely to see each one, and count carefully to ensure you haven't missed any.

After you've worked Row 1 of the Body, try the sweater on. It should end comfortably below the armpit. Remember, it will be at least another inch longer after blocking and after the rest of the Body is worked, adding the weight of the fabric. If it's way too short, you can add more rows, worked even.

You can also tell at this point whether the bust circumference is working. If it's too tight, you can make extra chains at the underarm; if too loose, make fewer chains. This is the reason it's wise to try on the sweater right after completing the first row of the Body. This allows you to make alterations before working more of the Body. Note that if you make this alteration on a design that has a stitch pattern, you'll want to be aware of the multiple so you can add or subtract the correct number of stitches to stay in pattern.

Raglan pullovers begin at the center back. They can either be worked in the round by using a connecting stitch at the end of the row, or they can be worked flat and seamed. If you've never done the connecting stitch, check out the recommended videos and give it a try. Raglan cardigans begin at the center front, and no seam is needed.

Except for the Regina coat and Zoey, all the designs are worked with no shaping in the Body. Those two designs expand the Body to create more fullness.

The length of any of these top-down designs is entirely up to you. You can work the Body to whatever length you prefer. Just remember that this will affect the amount of yarn needed. The lengths of Sleeves can also be easily adjusted.

After you've done the Body, it's time to work the garment's two Sleeves. Sleeves are best worked without a connecting stitch—in other words, worked flat. The main reason is that the hook cannot bend to accommodate the curve of the Sleeve. Though it can be done, it's clumsy and time-consuming. You work as far as you can; then when you can't progress further, you pull the hook through all the stitches made to this point and slide them onto the cable. This allows you to continue picking up forward row stitches. On the return row, similarly, you work off all the stitches on the hook as far as possible, then slide stitches from the cable back onto the hook and work them off. It's not so much fun to do row after row, and therefore I, for one, seldom use the connecting stitch on sleeves.

Even when working a Sleeve flat, you may need to use the strategy described above for a few rows at the beginning of the Sleeve. You can work about half the stitches, slide your hook through them, and work the other half. The exact number of stitches when making the switch is not important, but **pay attention to the tension of the stitch made right after sliding your stitches onto the**

cable. It can easily become enlarged as you work the next stitch. After sliding your hook to the cable, when continuing on to the next stitch, keep that stitch tight and check that the adjacent loop on the cable isn't stretching too much. After working a few rows of the Sleeve, you will find you can work flat, as there is more distance from the curved armhole.

As you tackle the designs here, remember these steps as you go through the patterns and work each section. Remember to keep measuring and trying on. Once all the sweater's main fabric has been crafted, it's time to put on the finishing touches.

Other Top-Down Options

In two top-down designs here—Frida and Zoey—we did not use raglan shaping. The advantage is that the neckline is rounded, unlike raglans where the neckline has corners. Stitches are still added as you work the yoke but not at marked raglan points. The precise shaping methods are explained further in each pattern.

FINISHING

Finishing encompasses everything that happens after the main fabric has been completed, including seams, edgings, blocking, placing buttons, and making buttonholes. If you do these things well, your sweater will look great. You want to really pay attention to detail so that all the work you've already done gets to truly shine.

Weaving in ends can also be considered part of finishing. It's easy to do in the close fabric of most Tunisian garments. Where stitches are more open, you'll need to weave ends in with particular care so that they are unobtrusive and will stay put. Make sure to change direction as you weave in so that the yarn is less likely to wriggle its way out.

I often do not weave in the very first and last stitch of work, because it can be helpful to see those when I'm blocking—those tails can help you identify the precise spot where a section started or ended.

Edgings

The term "edging" refers to stitches worked into the top, bottom, or side edges of your work. After the main fabric of your project is done, there may or may not be a need for this kind of finish on any edges. Sometimes edgings are very functional, as when we edge a neckline or the bottom of a sleeve to tighten them up. Other times they are purely decorative, providing an inch or two of contrasting fabric to make the main fabric pop.

Since neckline edging is used often in this book, let's start there. If you're edging a bottom-up sweater, the edging is worked into your last row of work. On a top-down sweater, neckline edging is worked into the foundation chain. In both cases, since often the point is to provide a closer fit at the neckline, you may be instructed to use a smaller hook. When you've done the first row of neckline edging, go ahead and try on your sweater to see if you need even more tightening. If you do, you can work subsequent rows, making a few decreases as you go, perhaps four or five per row.

The same is true when edging is used at the bottom of a sleeve. Work the first row, try on your garment, and decide whether the fit is as snug or loose as you like. Don't try to remove too many stitches in one row, or your fabric may bunch up. It's particularly important to pay attention to your tension on edging rows; otherwise the fabric may pucker or spread.

Wherever you are working your edging, it's wise to insert your hook under two loops for stability. Exactly which two loops you pick up is not so important as long as you are consistent throughout so that the entire edge looks the same. This is true whether the edging is worked in Tunisian or regular crochet. There are times when only one loop is available, but there's no cause for concern when that is the case. In some patterns, instructions for picking up stitches for edgings are very detailed in order to produce the neatest result.

Most cardigans have edgings on each Front piece along the center. That means your stitches are worked into row-ends, making it a bit trickier than working into the first or last row of work. Here, too, insert your hook under two strands of yarn when possible. Cardigan edgings usually begin at the bottom of one Front piece, then continue to the top and around the entire neckline, then keep going to the second Front piece all the way to its bottom. This requires working your way around some corners, so there will be increases and decreases as you work these edgings. Many of them use single crochet stitches, which I find contrast with Tunisian crochet in a very attractive way. The density of single crochet is also a plus for lending stability to your garment. You'll also find Tss and Tks used for edgings on some designs.

Seams

You need not be an expert sewer to seam your crochet garments well. The scale of yarn versus sewing thread makes it much easier. My sewing skills are limited, and the methods I am recommending work for my purposes. If you are more skilled and prefer to handle any of these sewing tasks differently, do not hesitate to do so!

Seams can be either sewn with a tapestry needle or joined with a crochet hook. The latter creates a stronger seam, and for that reason it's my choice for joining the shoulders when working bottom-up garments. There is considerable pull downward from the weight of the garment, and a strong, stable seam is desirable.

I have spelled out how I made the seams in most patterns. In most cases I used a slip stitch across the garment's shoulders and a sewn seam to connect the Body of the garment either at the side or at the center back. The sewn seam was also used to join the Sleeves at their center from the underarm to the wrist.

To work a slip stitch seam joining Front and Back shoulder, join yarn either at the neck edge or shoulder edge. Insert your hook under one or two strands from the front and one or two strands from the back, and pull the yarn through the loop on your hook. Inserting under two loops on both sides makes the seam stronger. Use this when the garment is fairly heavy. One loop on each side will be fine for a lighter weight garment. This will depend a lot on the fibers used in your yarns.

I find a smaller hook is easier to work with for slip stitch seams, but the size of the hook does not dictate my tension. Rather, I am striving to match the tension of the stitches I'm working into and to make sure the shoulder edges don't tighten or enlarge.

When seaming a sleeve or the back of a pullover, I use a sewn seam. This method is less obtrusive. It can be hard to create a completely invisible seam, and if you think about it, we are used to visible seams in all manufactured clothing. What we're aiming for in our seams is for them to be neat and tidy.

Join yarn at one end of the seam. Insert your needle between the two loops of the first stitch at the edge, work the needle through, and bring it up through two loops of the following stitch on the same side. Now do the exact same thing on the second side: needle down through two loops of the first stitch, up through two loops of the second stitch. Depending on how large the stitches are, you can include some other strands of yarn from the edge of the return pass as you work your needle through stitches. That's a good thing; it will make the seam more stable.

When executing this sewn seam, you want to match stitch for stitch as you work along row edges. This can be trickier than you think! If you recall, Tunisian crochet can be problematic in creating somewhat uneven side edges. Most of that issue can be taken care of with blocking. If there is still a small difference in length between one side of the seam and the other, it can be eliminated by sewing the seam carefully.

I highly recommend loosely pinning the two sides of the seam with safety pins at intervals of about 5 in./13 cm to keep yourself on track. Match stitch for stitch on each side. If the stitches on the starting edge are a bit larger (as they often are), they will be eased in as you sew to the final edge.

After making any seams, you can always make them look flatter and nicer by steaming them a little—just hover your steam iron over the seam for a minute, and you should be good.

Sweater Fit and Construction

Button Bands and Buttons

The cardigans in this book have center front edgings. When the design is meant to close with buttons, one side of the edging will be used to sew the buttons on, the other side to create matching buttonholes. The main concern when doing these button bands is precise placement of the button and the buttonhole.

When selecting buttons, think about the size and color and whether you want the buttons to stand out or blend into the background. You want to avoid heavy buttons that will pull crochet fabric out of shape. I've used both shanked and unshanked buttons. Shanks can make it easier to sew the button onto crochet fabric.

Some of these button bands are done with single crochet stitches, others with a Tunisian stitch. In either case, the buttonhole is created by skipping a stitch. In regular crochet you will chain 1 instead of working into the next stitch, and in Tunisian you will skip the stitch where the buttonhole is and do a chain 1 in that spot on the return pass. All this is spelled out in each pattern.

I recommend working the right button band first—that's the side the buttons will be sewn onto. Once you've done that, spread your buttons out at even intervals along the band. They can start quite close to the neck and should not be too far apart. To be sure they are equidistant, count the rows between buttons. Mark the spots you intend to sew buttons to. You can have a few inches at the bottom of the band with no button.

Sew the buttons on by either using your original yarn or sewing thread in a similar color. If the yarn is too thick, you can unply it to get a thinner strand. With a shanked button, work from the wrong side of the garment. Run your needle through fabric on one side of the button, then through the shank, and then through the fabric on the other side. All this should be kept very close to the button. Repeat seven or eight times to secure the button to the fabric.

If using unshanked buttons with two or four holes, work from the right side. Insert your needle into one hole all the way through to the wrong side, then bring the needle up into the adjacent hole. Repeat several times. If you have four holes, do this twice.

Now work the second button band, placing holes in the exact same row as the button on the other side. I like to check that the button and hole align as I make the band, so I'll make the first buttonhole, stop work, and test that the button and its hole are well aligned by closing the button. Then I do the next buttonhole.

Blocking

Artful blocking is all about getting just the right degree of stretch to have the exact fabric you want with the precise dimensions you require.

There are two things to be mindful of when blocking sweaters. One is to consider carefully how the fiber will react to wet blocking. With alpaca, certain merinos, and bamboo, it's wise to avoid too much stretching. If your yarn is 100% of any of those fibers, use caution to avoid overstretching. Many yarns are blends and can be blocked quite precisely to the dimensions you need. I urge you to use a blocking board that has measurements on it, so you can get exactly the size sweater you intended.

It's quite educational to swatch any favorite yarn with the same stitch and to try blocking it more or less heavily. Sometimes a minimal blocking, where the fabric is not drenched but merely spritzed with water, produces a great result; other times, a fabric can look better the more you stretch it. This is a big part of the art of crochet fabric making, and I encourage you to experiment and play. Put your practice swatches to use here!

Since natural fibers can react dramatically when fully immersed in water, I tend to be cautious when wet blocking, and I spritz them with water instead of soaking them. For long-term care of items made with natural fibers, I dry clean rather than wash them. I do use water to clean any small spots when necessary. The point is not that water is harmful to natural fibers but that when large pieces are very wet, they can stretch a lot, something we clearly want to avoid.

Spritz your item on both sides, covering all areas without drenching. Spread your work out on a blocking board large enough to accommodate the required measurements. Gently spread the work as needed to match measurements. Check the measurements for your size on the sweater's schematic. If you want to adjust those measurements more precisely for your body, you can usually add an inch or two with blocking.

Since blocking boards are only so large, I block sweaters in sections when possible. A cardigan can easily be blocked in sections, doing one Front piece, then the Back, then the other Front. For a pullover, you can block the Body before seaming. If you use a connecting stitch, you will be blocking the Front and Back at the same time, one on top of the other.

Begin pinning along a top or bottom edge, working your way down one side. The process of gently "massaging" your work into the proper size can take several minutes. As you pin one portion, stretch another, and gradually have all the fabric pinned to the blocking board. Look at your stitches and see that they are as well aligned as possible. The aim is to have the fabric evenly spread across the whole piece being blocked. You don't want bunching of fabric in the center or stretching at the edges.

If you're blocking the Front and Back at the same time for a pullover, make sure the fabric at the bottom is being stretched to the same degree as the fabric that you can see. I recommend you let the top fabric partially dry, then flip the garment over, repin, and allow the other side to dry.

Pay particular attention when blocking necklines, especially the V-necks in this collection, to be sure they measure and look the same on both sides.

When working with fragile fibers or those that can stretch too much, wet blocking can be avoided altogether. Instead, you can use a steam iron and steam out any curl in the fabric. Both wet blocking and steaming also soften the fabric, making it nicer on the skin and more flexible on the body.

With very soft fibers like alpaca and pima cottons, I try to avoid blocking altogether. These fibers will stretch a bit with wear, so if your item starts a little snug, not to worry. Both Nola and Joni came off the hook with no further blocking needed.

WHERE SHOULD I BEGIN?

If you're new to sweater making, I'd recommend beginning with the first two designs: Nola and Mimi. Both are sleeveless, are worked from the bottom up, and use uncomplicated stitches. Both require some shaping in the yoke and will therefore give you experience with marking and counting stitches, working left and right sides symmetrically, seaming, and working trim. They are a great starting point for your skill building, and the garments are versatile classics.

Once you're comfortable with the basics, move on to another of the bottom-up designs in the first part of the design collection. Each has its own challenges and offers opportunities to further refine your skills, whether with a new stitch, a colorwork or finishing technique, or shaping a sleeve or neckline.

If you're a fan of Tunisian simple stitch, take a look at Gilliam, an easygoing sweater that's straightforward to make. Or you might want to tackle a challenging color project like Aimee or learn the fabulous stitches featured in Layla, Becca, Nina, and Tina. It's all about what kind of challenge you'd like for your next step.

When you feel ready, move on to the top-down designs in the latter half. All these garments follow a similar formula of increasing throughout the yoke. Some are shaped as raglans, some are not.

In either case, technical challenges include using markers and counting stitches. A good starting point is Joni, a short-sleeved option using worsted weight yarn that will go quickly. To continue your journey with raglan shaping, you might choose Vanessa next, where there are several stitches in the raglan line. Becca offers a similar challenge, as well as the chance to make a button band worked as trim. Regina is a bigger project that includes A-line body shaping and a button band worked as part of the main fabric.

The two non-raglan options are each quite interesting. Zoey features a great puff stitch and works up quickly, while Frida is an excellent way to use up your stash of worsted weight yarns.

Have you added a sufficient number of new sweaters to your wardrobe? Well then, you might want to tackle a skirt—and we have one called Tess, the companion to Vanessa. It is made top down with regular increases at markers, so it's technically very similar to what we've been doing on other top-down garments.

Don't forget to enjoy your journey! Keep in mind that it's all about building skills and gaining confidence. Errors should be expected. Sometimes you may have to frog. Gauge can be elusive. As in many other aspects of life, mastery comes from overcoming obstacles. Just keep in mind that challenges are not enemies, they are teachers. Take notes, record your thoughts about the process, show off your finished objects. Making and finishing your own garments can be a source of real joy and a tremendous sense of accomplishment. Once you've made one sweater, you'll want to make many more!

3 | Patterns

Nola is a neat, practical vest. It is worked from the bottom up and flat, with shaping for a fitted armhole. After finishing the Body, the Front and Back Yokes are worked separately. There is a seam at the side of the body and seams at each shoulder. Gentle stripes on the body are matched by trim around armholes and neckline.

Tunisian knit stitch has the great appeal of looking like knitting, yet it is also a dense stitch. For that reason, I chose a yarn with high alpaca content. Alpaca is one of the softest and squishiest fibers of all, and it's also very warm. Cascade Yarn's Eco Highland yarn is undyed, and the natural, neutral colors are perfect for a wardrobe staple that blends well with other colors. Use a soft and squishy light worsted weight yarn for best results.

FINISHED BUST MEASUREMENTS

Sizes 1 through 5.

34.5 (38.5, 42.5, 46.5, 52) in./87.5 (98, 108, 118, 132) cm

Suggested ease: 0–4 in./0–10 cm

Note: Dimensions on schematic are before trim is added. This will assist you when blocking your work. Trim is 0.5 in./13 mm wide, so it will add a total of 1 in./2.5 cm to the shoulder width and make the armhole 0.5 in./13 mm smaller.

MATERIALS
- Cascade Yarns Eco Highland Duo; 70% baby alpaca, 30% merino; 197 yds./180 m per 3.5 oz./100 g; light worsted; Cafe Au Lait (A): 2 (2, 3, 3, 4) balls, Ecru (B): 1 (2, 2, 2, 3) balls
- Suggested hook sizes:
    - L-11 (8.0 mm) cabled Tunisian hook
    - J-10 (6.0 mm) cabled Tunisian hook (for trim only)
- 2 stitch markers

GAUGE

12 sts and 14 rows in Tks = 4 in./10 cm with larger hook

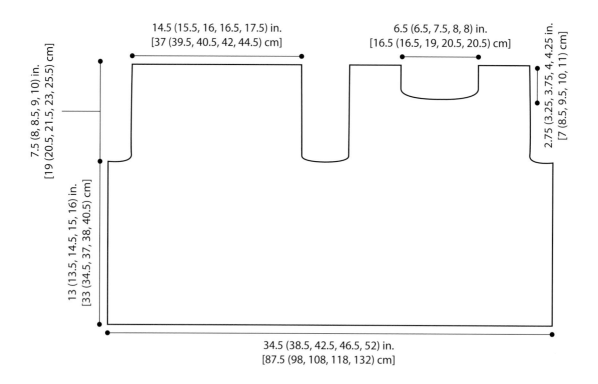

SPECIAL STITCHES AND ABBREVIATIONS

Work 2 Tks stitches together (Tks2tog): Insert hook in next st as in Tss, then into following st as in Tks, draw loop through both sts.

Tunisian slip stitch (Tsl sl): Insert hook as in Tss, draw loop through st and loop on hook. Work loosely to match these closing loops to your overall gauge. This stitch is used instead of Tks on last row of garment to avoid curled edge.

Tks sl st: Insert hook as in Tks, draw loop through st and loop on hook. This is used on last row of trim. The natural curl is part of the finished look.

SEVEN ROW STRIPE PATTERN

1 row B, 1 row A, 3 rows B, 1 row A, 1 row B

Note: When working this stripe pattern, the unused yarn can be carried along the side of the work until it's needed. There will be a short visible strand of color A on the inside of the work. When finished with all 7 rows, cut yarn B.

BODY

With larger hook and A, ch 104 (116, 128, 140, 156) sts.

Work Basic Foundation Row. All Rtn rows worked in usual manner.

Rows 2–14 (2–16, 2–16, 2–16, 2–20): Tks across.
Rows 15–21 (17–23, 17–23, 17–23, 21–27): Work stripe pattern. Change to color A.
Rows 22–27 (24–30, 24–30, 24–32, 28–36): Tks across.
Rows 28–34 (31–37, 31–37, 33–39, 37–43): Work stripe pattern. Change to color A.
Rows 35–45 (38–48, 38–50, 40–52, 44–56): Tks across, end off.

YOKE

Divide for Front and Back

Count 52 (58, 64, 70, 78) sts and PM in this st. This marks the last stitch of Front. Front and Back have same number of sts. Back yoke is worked first, then Front yoke.

Back Yoke

With Back facing, join yarn in st after M.

Row 1: Tsl st over next 2 (3, 4, 5, 6) sts, Tks2tog, cont in patt to 5 (6, 7, 8, 9) sts before last st, Tks2tog, end st, leave rem sts unworked. 46 (50, 54, 58, 64) sts

Row(s) 2 (2–3, 2–4, 2–5, 2–7): Tks2tog, cont in patt across to last 3 sts, Tks2tog, end st, ending with 44 (46, 48, 50, 52) sts.

Rows 3–26 (4–28, 5–30, 6–32, 8–35): Tks across.

Work Tsl st across, end off.

Front Yoke

Join yarn in first st of Front.

Rows 1–16 (1–17, 1–17, 1–18, 1–20): Follow instructions for Back.

Left Neckline Shaping

Row 17 (18, 18, 19, 21): Tks in next 10 (11, 11, 11, 12) sts, Tks2tog, leave rem sts unworked, work Rtn row. 12 (13, 13, 13, 14) sts

Rows 18–26 (19–28, 19–30, 20–32, 22–35): Tks across. 26 (28, 30, 32, 35) rows at armhole

Work Tss sl st across, end off.

Right Neckline Shaping

Returning to row 16 (17, 17, 18, 20), count 13 (14, 14, 14, 15) sts from end of row, join yarn in this st.

Row 17 (18, 18, 19, 21): Tks2tog, Tks across. 12 (13, 13, 13, 14) sts

Rows 18–26 (19–28, 19–30, 20–32, 22–35): Tks across.

Tss sl st across, end off.

FINISHING

Weave in all ends and block. Front and Back can be blocked separately.

Work side seam.

On last row of Back, count 12 (13, 13, 13, 14) sts from each shoulder edge and PM. Sew shoulder seams using these M to match Front shoulder stitches.

Armhole Trim
With smaller hook, join B at shoulder seam. Draw up bottom loop of each row-end around entire sleeve opening and in each st at underarm, work Rtn row.

Next row: Tks across.

Next row: Tks sl st around, end off. Use long tail to sew edges of trim together.

Neckline Trim
With smaller hook, join B at neckline edge of right shoulder seam. Working into different sections of neckline, do as follows:

On Back, pick up BL; along left shoulder, pick up outermost loop; on Front, work Tks; on right shoulder, pick up BL; on remainder of Back, pick up BL; work Rtn row.

Work 2 rows of Tks, then Tks sl st across, end off. Use long tail to sew edges of trim together.

Mimi is a V-neck cardigan/vest that can be worn on its own or as a coverup. It's worked bottom up with no armhole shaping. Neck shaping on the two front pieces creates the V-neck. Honeycomb stitch is featured in this design. It is trimmed with regular single crochet stitches, and three little buttons are used to close the front.

Honeycomb stitch is one of the prettiest Tunisian stitches. Because it uses Tunisian simple stitch and Tunisian purl, it has great drape and also lovely texture. The combo can't be beat! For this summery garment, I sought a yarn with some cotton and found Universal's Bamboo Pop just right, as the blend of cotton and bamboo fiber yields a nice drape. After swatching with different-sized hooks, I chose a fairly small one because it gave the fabric crisp definition. It's always a matter of balancing elements!

FINISHED BUST MEASUREMENTS
Sizes 1 through 5.

33.5 (37.5, 42, 46.5, 51) in./85 (95.5, 106.5, 118, 129.5) cm

Suggested ease: 0–3 in./0–7.5 cm

MATERIALS
- Universal Yarn Bamboo Pop; 50% bamboo, 50% cotton; 292 yds./267 m per 3.5 oz./100 g; sport weight*; True Red #136: 3 (3, 4, 4, 5) balls

It is classified as DK, but in my experience (and confirmed by online discussion I've read), it is closer to sport weight.

- Suggested hook sizes:
  - G-6 (4.0 mm) cabled Tunisian hook
  - F-5 (3.75 mm) regular crochet hook (for trim)
- Three 4 in./8.5 cm diameter shanked buttons

GAUGE
13 sts and 13 rows in patt = 3 in./7.5 cm

Honeycomb Stitch Pattern
Row 1: *Tss in next st, Tps in next st, rep from * across.

Row 2: *Tps in Tss, Tss in Tps, rep from * across.

Rep Rows 1 and 2 for patt.

Note: In instructions below, there is an odd number of stitches so that pattern is symmetrical.

BODY
Ch 145 (161, 181, 201, 221) sts.

Row 1: Work foundation row.
Rows 2 and 3: Tss across.
Row 4: Begin Honeycomb patt.

Continue in patt working *a total of* 56 (57, 58, 59, 60) rows. Check the length on the schematic, and if you prefer a longer garment, you can work additional rows here before working Yoke.

YOKE
Divide for Front and Back
*Count 36 (40, 45, 50, 55) sts from beg of next row and PM in this st. Now, beginning at the end of the row, rep from *. You have marked out 36 (40, 45, 50, 55) sts on each Front piece. You should have 73 (81, 91, 101, 111) sts on Back.

Back Yoke
Join yarn in st after first M. Work in patt to st before 2nd M. 73 (81, 91, 101, 111) sts

Work in patt for 29 (31, 33, 35, 39) rows.

Last row: Inserting hook in patt, work Tsl st across, end off.

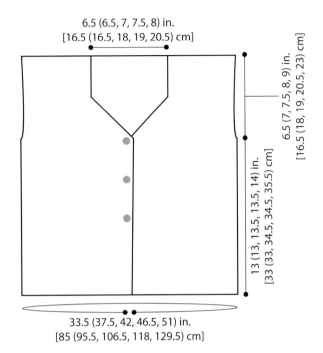

6.5 (6.5, 7, 7.5, 8) in.
[16.5 (16.5, 18, 19, 20.5) cm]

6.5 (7, 7.5, 8, 9) in.
[16.5 (18, 19, 20.5, 23) cm]

13 (13, 13.5, 13.5, 14) in.
[33 (33, 34.5, 34.5, 35.5) cm]

33.5 (37.5, 42, 46.5, 51) in.
[85 (95.5, 106.5, 118, 129.5) cm]

Right Front Yoke with Neckline Shaping
Continue working on the unused sts of last row on Body. Join yarn in first st.

Row 1: Work in patt across to first M, work end st in M. 36 (40, 45, 50, 55) sts
Row 2: Tss2tog, cont in patt across. 35 (39, 44, 49, 54) sts

Note: This decrease is used regardless of st patt.

Rows 3–15 (3–15, 3–16, 3–17, 3–18): Rep Row 2 13 (13, 14, 15, 16) more times, ending with 22 (26, 30, 34, 38) sts.

Work 14 (16, 17, 18, 21) more rows even in patt. You should have *a total of* 29 (31, 33, 35, 39) rows on Yoke.

Last row: Inserting hook in patt, work Tsl st across, end off.

Left Front Yoke with Neckline Shaping

Join yarn in 2nd M, draw up loop.

Row 1: Work in patt across.
Row 2: Work in patt to last 3 sts, Tss2tog, end st. PM in last st. (This M will be used when creating buttonhole on trim.)

Rep from Row 3 of Right Front.

Work 14 (16, 17, 18, 21) more rows even in patt. You should have a *total of* 29 (31, 33, 35, 39) rows on Yoke.

Last row: Inserting hook in patt, work Tsl st across, end off.

FINISHING

You may wish to block work before joining shoulders and working Trim.

Join front and back Shoulders.

On Back, *count 22 (26, 30, 34, 38) sts, PM in this st. Now beg at end of row, rep from *. This will allow you to be precise when seaming shoulders. This should leave 29 (29, 31, 33, 35) sts for the Back neck. Matching stitch for stitch on Front and Back shoulders, with WS facing, work slip stitch seam inserting hook under 2 loops of Front and 2 loops of Back.

Center Front and Neckline Trim

Join yarn in lower right (left for left-handers) corner of front.

With regular crochet hook, ch 1, sc in each row-end, taking care to match your tension to the size of the stitches you are working into. The tension will vary as you work your way around: looser working into the slanted sts at the V-neck and tighter working into the top edge of the back neck. Move M up to sc worked into marked row-end. Turn at end of row.

On next row we create buttonholes on garment left front. Move M down 1 row. (Count 11 sts, PM in next st) twice. You should have 3 markers placed for buttonholes. The buttonhole is a simple ch-1.

Next row: Ch 1, sc in each sc across working ch-1 instead of sc at each M, working all around neckline to opposite Front corner, turn.
Next row: Ch 1, sc across working into ch-1 sp of buttonholes where needed, end off.

If needed, block trim before sewing on buttons.

Sew buttons to 2nd row of trim on Right Front to match buttonholes.

Aimee

Aimee is a colorful, sporty pullover with an interesting stitch pattern. The fit is meant to be fairly close, with a small armhole that minimizes the extra fabric in the dropped-shoulder construction. In this four-color version, follow the stripe pattern carefully. Or if you prefer to keep things simple, it will work beautifully made all in one color, or perhaps two with a simpler striping pattern.

The yarn used, HiKoo Sueño, is very stretchy, and while listed as a DK, it is on the light side of this yarn weight. Note that it is a mix of merino—the softest kind of wool—and bamboo, a fiber that enhances fluidity as well. The stitch pattern used is also one that promotes this quality, as there are open spaces in the fabric.

STITCH PATTERN NOTES

An upside down shell is an interesting feature of the stitch pattern. The shells alternate with 3 Tss stitches. This requires a different Rtn row than the Basic Rtn row. On the Rtn row, after the initial chain and (yo, draw through 2 loops), we bring the hook through 4 loops to make the shell. We then make a chain, then bring the hook through 2 loops 3 times for the next 3 Tss, then another chain.

On forward rows, a Tfs is worked on either side of these shells, and we also work into the chain atop the shell. For the first Tfs, insert the hook under the Rtn row between a Tss and the next shell. You'll then see a small loop above the shell—insert the hook in that loop. For the second Tfs, insert the hook under the Rtn row between the shell and the next Tss. Continue working Tss as usual until the next shell.

The pattern repeat consists of the shell, which has 3 stitches, plus 3 Tss, therefore 6 stitches in total.

Tfs stitches worked on both sides of a shell

Return row worked up to shell

Return row worked including shell

Chain 1 on Return row

FINISHED BUST MEASUREMENTS

Sizes 1 through 5.

33 (36, 42, 48, 54) in./84 (91.5, 106.5, 122, 137) cm

Suggested ease: 0–3 in./0–7.5 cm

MATERIALS

- HiKoo Sueño; 80% merino, 20% viscose from bamboo; 255 yds./233 m per 3.5 oz./100 g; DK weight; 2 (2, 3, 3, 3) skeins each of Evergreen #1145 (A), Mountain Fog #1202 (B), Indigo #1135 (C), Sage #1201 (D)
- Suggested hook sizes:
    - J-10 (6.0 mm) cabled Tunisian hook
    - G-6 (4.0 mm) regular crochet hook (for seam only)

GAUGE

2 pattern repeats (12 sts) = 3 in./7.5 cm; 14 rows = 4 in./10 cm

Gauge Swatch

Ch 25.

Do not work usual foundation row.

Row 1 Fwd: Draw up loop in each ch. **Rtn:** Yo, draw through 1 loop, yo, draw through 2 loops, *ch 1, yo, draw through 4 loops, ch 1**, (yo, draw through 2 loops) 3 times, rep from * ending last rep at **, (yo, draw through 2 loops) 2 times. (4 pattern repetitions + 1 end st)

Row 2 Fwd: Tss, *Tfs, draw up loop in closing ch of fan, Tfs**, 3 Tss, rep from * across ending last rep at **, Tss, end st. **Rtn:** Rep Row 1 Rtn.

Rep Row 2 until you have *a total of* 21 rows. Tss sl st across, end off.

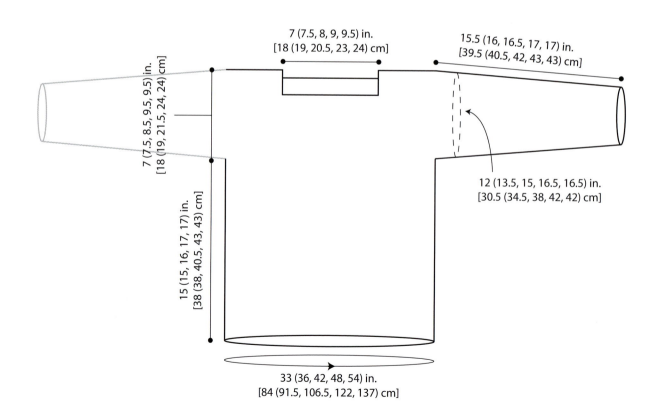

The Tunisian Crochet Sweater Collection

SPECIAL STITCHES AND ABBREVIATIONS

Tss decrease (Tss2tog): Insert hook in next 2 bars, draw up loop.

Decrease at beg of row: Tss2tog at start of row.

Decrease at end of row: Work to last 3 sts, Tss2tog, end st.

BODY

With A, ch 133 (145, 169, 193, 217) sts.

Do not work usual foundation row.

Row 1 Fwd: Draw up loop in each ch. **Rtn:** Yo, draw through 1 loop, yo, draw through 2 loops, *ch 1, yo, draw through 4 loops, ch 1**, (yo, draw through 2 loops) 3 times, rep from * ending last rep at **, (yo, draw through 2 loops) 2 times. 22 (24, 28, 32, 36) pattern repetitions + 1 end st

Row 2 Fwd: Tss, *Tfs, draw up loop in closing ch of fan, Tfs**, 3 Tss, rep from * across ending last rep at **, Tss, end st. **Rtn:** Rep Row 1 Rtn.
Rep Row 2 for patt.

Following the stripe patt below, work in patt for 53 (53, 56, 59, 59) rows.

Color A: 11 (11, 12, 13, 13) rows. This includes 2 rows already worked.
Color B: 2 rows
Color A: 2 rows
Color B: 2 rows
Color C: 2 rows
Color B: 2 rows

From this point on, for simplicity, we will give only letter names for colors.

C: 6 (6, 7, 8, 8) rows
D: 2 rows
C: 2 rows
D: 2 rows
B: 2 rows
D: 2 rows

B: 6 (6, 7, 8, 8) rows
A: 2 rows
B: 2 rows
A: 2 rows
D: 2 rows
A: 2 rows

Divide for Front and Back
Count 11 (12, 14, 16, 18) Fans from start of row. Sk next Tss, PM in next Tss.

This marks the edge between garment Front and Back. The marked st will be used on both Front and Back.

67 (73, 85, 97, 109) sts each on Front and Back.

Back Yoke
Following the stripe patt below, work in patt to M for 22 (25, 28, 31, 31) rows.

D: 11 (12, 14, 14, 14) rows
C: 2 rows
D: 2 rows
C: 7 (9, 10, 13, 13) rows

Back Right Shoulder
Cont working with Color C.

Next row: Work in patt over 19 (19, 25, 25, 31) sts, Tss in next 0 (2, 1, 5, 4) sts, leave rem sts unworked.
Next row: Work in patt over these sts.

You should have a *total of* 24 (27, 30, 33, 33) rows.

Tss sl st across, end off.

Back Left Shoulder
Beg at end of row, count 19 (21, 26, 30, 35) sts. Join yarn in this st.

Next row: Tss in next 0 (2, 1, 5, 4) sts, cont in patt on rem sts across.
Next row: Work in patt over these sts.

Tss sl st across, end off.

Front Yoke
Matching color used at start of Back Yoke, join yarn in M (the same st as last st of Back).

Follow instructions for Back for 18 (20, 22, 24, 24) rows.

Left Shoulder
Continue with Color C only.

Next 6 (7, 8, 9, 9) rows: Work in patt over 19 (19, 25, 25, 31) sts. Tss in next 0 (2, 1, 5, 4) sts.

You should have a *total of* 24 (27, 30, 33, 33) rows.

Tss sl st across, end off.

Right Shoulder
Starting at end of last row of Body, count back 19 (19, 25, 25, 31) sts. Join C in this st. Follow instructions for Back Left Shoulder. Do not remove M.

Seam Shoulders
With RS facing, use regular hook to make sl st seam at shoulders.

Insert hook under 1 strand of both Front and Back, yo and draw up loop (sl st made),*insert hook in adjacent strand on both Front and Back, work sl st, rep from * across, end off. Rep on opposite Shoulder.

SLEEVES
Join Color B in M.

Row 1: Fwd: Draw up loop in each row-end around armhole. **Rtn:** Work in patt across. 49 (55, 61, 67, 67) sts

Work in pattern for 32 (32, 33, 34, 34) rows, changing color as follows:
B: 2 rows
D: 2 rows
Rep last 4 rows once.

B: 2 rows
A: 12 (12, 13, 14, 14) rows
D: 2 rows
C: 2 rows
Rep last 4 rows once.

D: 2 rows

Sleeve Shaping

Before we can work decreases, we must turn the shells at the edges into Tss. This is what occurs on the next row. Decreasing begins on the row after that. On all following rows, work Tss at edges instead of shells. Follow Stripe Pattern at right.

Row 33 (33, 34, 35, 35): Work Fwd as usual. **Rtn:** Yo, draw through 1 loop, (yo, draw through 2 loops) 7 times, *ch 1, yo, draw through 4 loops, ch 1, (yo, draw through 2 loops) 3 times, rep from * to last 5 sts, (yo, draw through 2 loops) 5 times.

Row 34 (34, 35, 36, 36) (Decrease row): Dec at beg and end of row. 47 (53, 59, 65, 65) sts

Row(s) 35–37 (35–36, 36, 37, 37): Work even in patt.

Row 38 (37, 37, 38, 38): Rep row 34 (34, 35, 36, 36): 45 (51, 57, 63, 63) sts

Rows 39–50 (38–52, 38–51, 39–56, 39–56): Rep last 4 (3, 2, 2, 2) rows 3 (5, 7, 9, 9) more times ending with 39 (41, 43, 59, 61) sts.

Work even for rem 3 (1, 6, 3, 1) row(s).

55 (56, 58, 60, 60) rows; ending with 39 (41, 43, 45, 45) sts.

Tss sl st across, end off.

Stripe Pattern

B: 11 (12, 13, 14, 14) rows
C: 2 rows
D: 2 rows
C: 2 rows
D: 2 rows
C: 2 rows
D: 2 rows

FINISHING

Block as needed. Sew sleeve seams.

Nina

Nina is part of a jacket/halter set, Nina and Tina—two pieces that work beautifully together, though each can stand alone. Nina features an attractive lace stitch that's easy (but do take the time to practice!) and fast, so you can complete the project quickly. An unusual feature of this design is that, rather than starting at the bottom and working in horizontal rows, it is worked vertically, meaning that rows run in a vertical direction extending from the hem to the shoulder.

Nina begins at the garment's center back. We work half the Back, then add chains for the Armhole, then continue working half the Front, incorporating neckline shaping. The second half begins by joining yarn in the first row of the first half. In other words, we begin again on the Back and work around to the Front.

The sleeves are worked directly into the armholes and are then seamed. Trim is added to the Front edges along with a cute little collar.

Sleeve worked into armhole

Berroco Pima Soft has been one of the best cottons for garments for years. Pima cotton is bred specifically for softness and can be found in manufactured clothing as well. This yarn has noticeable texture on the surface, which can sometimes compete with the clarity of stitches. That's why I chose stitches that are well defined. In the case of Nina, the openwork mesh declares itself boldly.

Center back

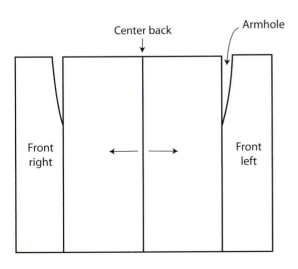

STITCH PATTERN NOTES

This stitch pattern uses a yarn over to create a stitch, something you may not have encountered before. Simply yarn over in the usual way, leave the strand of yarn on the hook, and insert the hook in the next stitch to work the Tks that follows the yarn over. When you work the return row, it will pass under this yarn over and you will see a slanted line that counts as a stitch.

Yarn over

Tks made after yarn over

This stitch has fabulous drape and works up super fast. But like certain Tunisian stitches, it has a tendency to slant to the right (or left for left-handers), and your fabric will have this slant coming off the hook. However, it can be completely blocked out so that the fabric lies flat and with proper alignment. For this reason, make sure your yarn responds to wet blocking. All natural fibers do, but some 100% acrylic yarns do not.

Nina

The stitch pattern begins with a Tks right after the first stitch of the row and ends with a Tks right before the end stitch of the row. The only place this is not the case in this pattern is on decrease rows at Front neckline.

FINISHED BUST MEASUREMENTS

Sizes 1 through 6.

34.5 (38.5, 42.5, 46.5, 50.5, 54.5) in./87.5 (98, 108, 118, 128.5, 138) cm

Suggested ease: 1–4 in./3–10 cm

MATERIALS

- Berroco Pima Soft, 100% Pima cotton; 124 yds./113 m per 1.75 oz./50 g; DK weight; Coral #4633 (A): 8 (9, 10, 12, 13, 15) balls, Ice #4608 (B): 1 (1, 1, 1, 2, 2) balls
- Suggested hook sizes:
  - J-10 (6.0 mm) cabled Tunisian hook
  - F-5 (3.75 mm) regular crochet hook (for trim)
- 2 stitch markers

GAUGE

16 sts and 12 rows = 4 in./10 cm

Sc gauge: 7 sts = 2 in./5 cm (for trim)

Mesh Stitch Gauge Swatch

Ch 25.

Row 1 Fwd: Draw up loop in 2nd ch, *yo, sk next ch, draw up loop in next ch, rep from * to last 2 sts, draw up loop in last 2 ch. **Rtn:** Yo, draw through 1 loop, *yo, draw through 2 loops, rep from * across.
Rows 2–19: *Tks in next st, yo, rep from * across ending with Tks in second to last st, end st.
All Rtn rows worked as in Row 1.

NOTES

It's easy to miss the 2nd st of the row, a Tks that tends to nestle very close to the first stitch. Pay special attention when starting rows.

There is no foundation row for this stitch. We begin the stitch pattern on the first row.

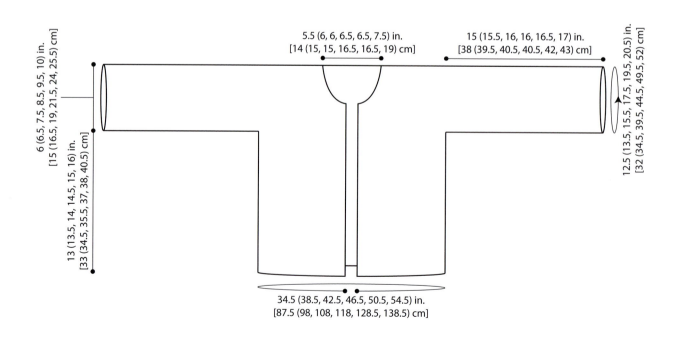

48   The Tunisian Crochet Sweater Collection

BODY LEFT

Ch 77 (81, 87, 93, 99, 105).

Row 1: Fwd: Draw up loop in 2nd ch, *yo, sk next ch, draw up loop in next ch, rep from * to last 2 sts, draw up loop in last 2 ch. **Rtn:** Yo, draw through 1 loop, *yo, draw through 2 loops, rep from * across. All Rtn rows worked as in Row 1. 77 (81, 87, 93, 99, 105) sts.

Row 2: *Tks in next st, yo, rep from * across ending with Tks in second to last st, end st.

Work in patt for a *total of* 26 (29, 32, 35, 38, 41) rows.

Nina

Left Armhole

Count 25 (27, 31, 35, 39, 41) sts from beg of row. Join yarn in this st by inserting hook under 2 loops of Rtn row just below yo.

Ch 25 (27, 31, 35, 39, 41). Now begin a new row by drawing up a loop in next ch, *yo, sk next ch, draw up loop in next ch, rep from * until end of added chains, yo, Tks in next Tks, cont in patt across. You should have 77 (81, 87, 93. 99, 105) sts.

Work in patt for a *total of* 18 (20, 23, 25, 28, 30) rows.

Front section in progress

Left Front with Neckline Shaping

The decreases for neckline are worked in the Rtn row by drawing the last loop through 3 loops, the loop on the hook and 2 sts. This eliminates 2 sts.

When you begin the Fwd row after the decrease, work in patt by working Tks in Tks after the decrease (with no yo before it) as in photo below at left.

Next row Fwd: Tsl st over next 7 (7, 9, 11, 11, 11) sts, cont in patt across. **Rtn:** Work usual Rtn to last 3 sts, yo, draw through 4 loops (makes 2-st dec). 68 (72, 76, 80, 86, 92) sts

Next 2 rows Fwd: Work in patt across. **Rtn:** Rep prev Rtn row, ending with 64 (68, 72, 76, 82, 88) sts.

Work even in patt for 5 (6, 6, 7, 7, 8) more rows.

BODY RIGHT

To begin Body Right, we work into Row 1 of Body Left. To work Tks into Row 1 of Body Left, insert hook into Row 1 Tks sts, which are upside down.

Join yarn in first st and draw up loop, *Tks, yo, rep from * across ending with Tks in 2nd to last st, end st.

Work a *total of* 26 (29, 32, 35, 38, 41) rows, place working loop on holder.

Right Armhole

The ends of rows are at the top of the garment. Count 25 (27, 31, 35, 39, 41) sts from end of prev row. This will bring you to the yarn over and chain of the Rtn pass. Join yarn by inserting hook under 2 loops of Rtn row, ch 25 (27, 31, 35, 39, 41), end off.

Next row: Work in patt to added chains, *yo, sk first ch, draw up loop in next ch, rep from * to last 2 ch, draw up loop in last 2 ch. You should have 77 (81, 87, 93. 99, 105) sts.

Work in patt for a *total of* 18 (20, 23, 25, 28, 30) rows, end off.

Right Front with Neckline Shaping

Beg at end of row, count 8 (8, 10, 12, 12, 12) sts. You should be at a Tks st. PM in this st. This eliminates 7 (7, 9, 11, 11, 11) sts.

The rem decreases for the neckline are worked in the Rtn row by drawing the first loop of the Rtn row through 3 stitches. This eliminates 2 stitches.

You will see these three gathered stitches. When you work the next Fwd row, skip the first two of these gathered stitches and insert your hook into the last of the three, work end stitch.

Work in patt to M, leave rem sts unworked. **Rtn:** Yo, draw through 3 loops, yo, draw through 2 loops, cont with usual Rtn row. 68 (72, 76, 80, 86, 92) sts

Next 2 rows Fwd: Work in patt across (see **Note**, page 48). **Rtn:** Rep prev Rtn row. 64 (68, 72, 76, 82, 88) sts

Work even for 5 (6, 6, 7, 7, 8) more rows, end off. 26 (29, 32, 35, 38, 41) rows total on each front.

Remove M.

Wet block to schematic measurements. I recommend doing Back section first, then Front pieces, making sure that necklines on each side are the same depth and width.

Work shoulder seams as follows:

Pin the Front and Back pieces together at shoulder, making sure to match the row-ends on the Back to those on the Front pieces. You want to use the same number of rows on Front and Back. There should be 16 (18, 18, 20, 20, 22) rows left between the shoulders for the Back neck. Seam shoulders together.

SLEEVES

When working around an armhole, you will find it hard to get all the way around, since the hook will not bend. After a few inches on the sleeve, this will cease to be an issue. But on the first few rows, when you are about halfway around, pull your hook all the way through the stitches made so that they are on the cable. Then continue to work the rest of the row. To make sure the stitch after this maneuver does not stretch out too much, give it a little tug before you proceed to the following stitch. On Rtn row you will again work about half the stitches off, then pull on the cable end to work off the remaining stitches.

Each sleeve should have 25 (27, 31, 35, 39, 41) sts each on Front and Back—a total of 50 (54, 62, 70, 78, 82) sts. To make the sleeve seamlessly, we join yarn at the bottom of sleeve opening and pick up stitches all around the sleeve. Note that you are continuing in pattern on both Front and Back, meaning the Tks will line up over the Tks on both sides. However, on one side you are working into the stitches upside down. Use your eye as a guide.

We are adding 2 stitches at the beg of sleeve in order to have a solid edge, **the first by working into the Rtn row, and the second by working under the Rtn row (as in Tfs)**. Follow the instructions below closely, and it will work out fine!

At bottom of armhole you will see a space before the first Tks. Insert hook in 2 strands of the Rtn row ch and draw up a loop, draw up next loop **under** Rtn row chains, yo, Tks in next Tks, cont in patt around sleeve to Tks before shoulder seam, sk shoulder seam, yo, Tks in first Tks after shoulder seam on opposite side, cont in patt to last Tks at bottom of armhole, draw up loop in last space. Work normal Rtn row. 51 (55, 63, 71, 79, 83) sts

Next row: Tks in next st, cont in patt across, Tks in 2nd to last st, end st.

Rep last row 44 (45, 46, 47, 48, 49) times or to desired length.

FINISHING
Trim on Front Edges

To work this trim, we must work into the Tks sts and also the yarnover sts. For the latter, simply insert your hook under the yo (which appears as a slanted strand wrapped around the Rtn row) and draw up a loop.

With regular hook, join yarn at bottom right front (left for left-handers). Ch 1, *(sc in next Tks, sc in next yo) twice, sc in next Tks, sk next yo, rep from * across to point where Front meets neckline shaping. Work 3 sc around corner and PM in center sc of inc. Sc in each row-end on rest of neckline and sc in each st across Back neckline, sc in each row-end on left Front neckline to corner, 3 sc in corner, PM in center st of inc just made, work opposite Front edge same as first side, turn.

Next 2 rows: Ch 1, *sc in each sc to M, 3 sc in M, move M to center sc of group just made, rep from * across. End off.

Collar

Join yarn in M.

Row 1: With regular crochet hook, ch 1, sc in each sc to next M, turn.

Next 10 (10, 12, 12, 12, 12) rows: Rep last row, end off.

Wet block sleeves to eliminate slant.

Wet block sc trim and collar to flatten. Use many pins to ensure it will hold shape.

Sew sleeve seam.

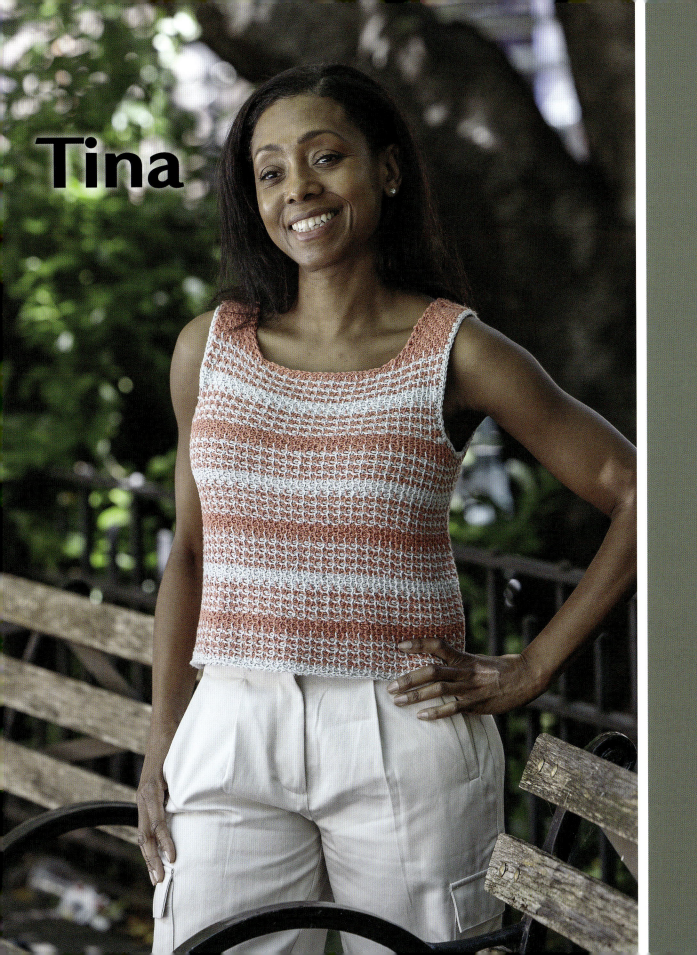

This halter is a fun piece that works great as a companion to Nina and can certainly have a life on its own too. It's worked bottom up with a fitted armhole. The garment's shoulders are a little narrower than full shoulder width, to allow a bit of exposure at the shoulders. The Front neck sits a little lower than the Back neck. The armhole is smaller than on a garment with sleeves so that undergarments are not exposed. Check the schematic for armhole depth against your measurements. Since this is worked bottom up, you can easily add an inch or two at the shoulders, if needed, by working a few additional rows on front and back shoulders before doing the short row shaping. This will give you a deeper armhole.

The halter body is meant to end a little below the waist. If you prefer it longer, the pattern includes a way to add 3 in./7.5 cm to the length. Check the schematic and your measurements to figure out what works best for you.

We use a less familiar stitch in this pattern that allows for an attractive checkered color pattern. It is called Tunisian slip stitch purled. In knitting, the term slip means to slip a stitch onto the needle without working it. That's what's done for this stitch. It starts like a Tunisian purl stitch: The yarn is brought forward, and we insert into the next vertical bar.

That bar is now on the hook and becomes part of the Fwd pass. Do not draw up a loop. Continue on to next stitch, a TSS, bringing yarn to back by moving your hook in front of yarn.

Note that in this case, the term "slip stitch" does not involve what crocheters normally think of with this term, that is, pulling the working loop through the loop on your hook. That's not what happens in this stitch. It's really quite an easy stitch to do, so please don't let the terminology get in your way.

Shoulder shaping is worked at the very top of the garment, adding a bit more fabric closer to the neck to account for the natural slope in the shoulder. If you'd prefer to skip this, however, you can create a similar effect when you block the sweater. Just stretch the fabric closer to the neck so it's about 0.5–1 in./1.5–2.5 cm longer than the shoulder edge.

The striping in this design involves alternating stripes of solid colors and mixed colors. You'll begin with a few rows in one color, then work a few rows alternating colors at the beginning of each forward pass, then work a few rows with the second color. The stripes with alternating colors are always larger than the solid-colored stripes.

As usual, this stitch benefits from loose tension. There is an important exception: When changing colors, work the first three stitches of the row tightly. This will help eliminate an enlarged first stitch.

For all color changes, yarn can be carried at the side. The unused color will span three rows of work and will appear on the inside of your garment. There's no need to cut yarn. Be attentive to your tension when carrying the color over several rows: As you make your first stitch, check that the yarn is stretched loosely over the intervening rows.

FINISHED BUST MEASUREMENTS

Sizes 1 through 6.

34 (38, 42.5, 46, 51) [86.5 (96.5, 108, 117, 129.5) cm]

Suggested ease: 1–4 in./3–10 cm

MATERIALS

- Berroco Pima Soft; 100% Pima cotton; 124 yds./113 m per 1.75 oz./50 g; DK weight; Coral #4633 (A): 3 (3, 4, 4, 5) balls, Ice #4608 (B): 2 (3, 3, 3, 4) balls
- Suggested hook sizes:
  - I-9 (5.5 mm) cabled Tunisian hook
  - G-6 (4.0 mm) regular crochet hook (for edging only)
- 2 stitch markers

GAUGE

11 sts = 3 in./7.5 cm; 16 rows = 4 in./10 cm

Gauge Swatch

Ch 22.

Work foundation row.

Row 1: *Tss, Tsl purled, rep from * across, end st.
Row 2: *Tsl purled, Tss, rep from * across, end st.

Repeat Rows 1 and 2 until you have *a total of* 24 rows.

SPECIAL STITCH AND ABBREVIATION

Tunisian slip stitch purled (Tsl purled): Bring yarn forward, insert hook in next bar but do not draw up loop, bring yarn to back. The bar from row below remains on the hook. Note that the term "slip" is used here as it is in knitting, not crochet. We are not making a crochet slip stitch, but rather, picking up a stitch from the previous row without working it.

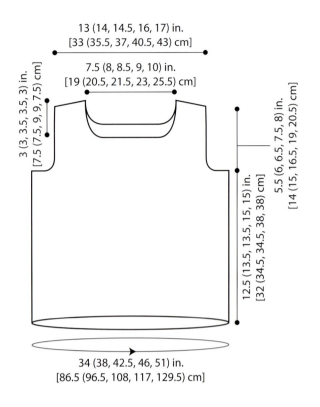

BODY

With B, ch 124 (140, 156, 168, 188).

Row 1: Work Basic Foundation Row.
Row 2: *Tss, Tsl purled, rep from * across, end st.
Row 3: *Tsl purled, Tss, rep from * across, end st.

Work in pattern for 0 (1, 1, 2, 2) more rows.

Change to A and work 7 rows in pattern, **alternating colors each forward row. Last row will be in A.

*Continuing with A, work 3 (4, 4, 5, 5) rows.

Change to B and work 7 rows **alternating colors each forward row**. Last row will be in B.

Rep from * working *a total of* 50 (55, 55, 60, 60) rows. Cont with A for Yoke.

If you would like a longer garment, you can begin with 3 (3, 4, 4, 5) rows of color A (including foundation row), then 7 rows alternating colors, then continue by making 3 (4, 5, 5, 5) rows of B. From there, follow the pattern beginning at **. This adds 2–3 in./5–7.5 cm to length. Note that the hem of your garment will be in color A, which is also at the halter's shoulders.

YOKE

Divide for Front and Back Yoke

Count 62 (70, 78, 84, 94) sts, PM in this st. There should be the same number of sts rem for Front Yoke (below).

Stripe Pattern:

3 (4, 4, 5, 5) rows in A.

Change to B and work 7 (7, 7, 7, 9) rows, alternating colors.

3 (4, 4, 5, 5) rows in B.

58 The Tunisian Crochet Sweater Collection

Change to A and work 7 (7, 7, 7, 9) rows, alternating colors.

3 (3, 5, 6, 5) rows in A.

You will have a *total of* 23 (25, 27, 30, 33) rows in Stripe pattern.

Back Yoke
Armhole Shaping
Work the above Stripe patt while at the same time shaping armhole as follows:

Row 1: Sl st over next 2 (3, 4, 5, 6) sts, cont in patt to 3 (4, 5, 6, 7) sts before M, work end st in nxt st, leave rem 2 (3, 4, 5, 6) sts on Back unworked. 58 (64, 70, 74, 82) sts.
Row 2: Tss2tog, cont in patt to last 3 sts, Tss2tog, end st. 56 (62, 68, 72, 80) sts.

Rep last row 4 (5, 7, 7, 9) more times, ending with 48 (52, 54, 58, 62) sts.

Work even until all rows of Stripe pattern are complete.

Back Right Shoulder
Note: Decreases are made on the Rtn pass. On the initial row below, to make a two-stitch decrease, we draw the hook through 3 loops. For the sake of neatness, on the following row when making the last st, insert the hook under all 3 of the loops at the edge and draw up a loop, treating the 3 loops as 1 st. After that we make one-stitch decreases on the Rtn row, which will not require this step. On the Fwd rows following those decreases, make an end st in the last st of the row.

Still working with A, *count 14 (15, 15, 16, 17) sts and PM. Beg at end of row, rep from *. These mark the inside edges of each shoulder.

Row 1 Fwd: Draw up loop in each st to M. **Rtn:** Yo, draw through 3 loops, *yo, draw through 2 loops; rep from * across. 12 (13, 13, 14, 15) sts

Row 2 Fwd: Work in patt across to last st, insert hook under all 3 sts decreased in prev row. **Rtn:** *Yo, draw through 2 loops, rep from * across. 11 (12, 12, 13, 14) sts
Row 3 Fwd: Work even across. **Rtn:** Rep last Rtn row. 10 (11, 11, 12, 13) sts
Rows 4–8: Work even across. Remove M.

Right Shoulder Shaping
Sl st over next 2 (3, 3, 3, 3) sts, cont in patt across. **Rtn:** Yo, draw through 1 loop, *yo, draw through 2 loops, rep from * until there are 3 loops on hook, yo, draw through 3 (3, 3, 3, 3) loops. 7 (7, 7, 8, 9) sts

Next row: Sl st over 3 (3, 3, 3, 4) sts, cont in patt across. **Rtn:** Rep last Rtn row. 3 (3, 3, 4, 4) sts

Tss sl st across.

Back Left Shoulder
Before making the shoulder, work Tsl st across unused sts between shoulders as follows: Join yarn in first M, sl st across to 2nd M, loop on hook is 1st st of next row.

Row 1 Fwd: Work in patt across. **Rtn:** Yo, draw through 1 loop, *yo, draw through 2 loops, rep from * until there are 4 loops on hook, yo, draw through 4 loops. 12 (13, 13, 14, 15) sts
Rows 2 and 3 Fwd: Work in patt across. **Rtn:** Yo, draw through 1 loop, *yo, draw through 2 loops, rep from * until there are 3 loops on hook, yo, draw through 3 loops. 10 (11, 11, 12, 13) sts
Rows 4–8: Work even.

Left Shoulder Shaping
Fwd: Work in patt over next 7 (7, 7, 8, 8) sts. **Rtn:** *Yo, draw through 2 loops, rep from * across. 7 (7, 7, 8, 8) sts
Next row Fwd: Work in patt over next 3 (3, 3, 4, 4) sts in patt. Rep last Rtn row. 3 (3, 3, 4, 4) sts

Tss sl st across next 9 (10, 10, 11, 12) sts on last 2 rows. 10 (11, 11, 12, 13) sts

Front Yoke

Join yarn in last st of back, sl st over the 2 (3, 4, 5, 6) unworked sts of back and over next 3 (4, 5, 6, 7) sts. 62 (70, 78, 84, 94) sts

Follow instructions for Back Yoke for 20 (22, 22, 26, 32) rows.

Front Right Shoulder

Follow instructions for Back Left Shoulder beg at Row 1 and up to Left Shoulder Shaping.

Work 3 (3, 5, 4, 1) more row(s) continuing with color A.

Follow instructions for Left Shoulder Shaping.

Left Shoulder

Follow instructions for Back Right Shoulder beg at Row 1 and up to Right Shoulder Shaping.

Work 3 (3, 5, 4, 1) more row(s), continuing with color A.

Follow instructions for Right Shoulder Shaping.

FINISHING

Block work to desired measurements before seaming.

Sew side seam.

Armhole Edging

With regular crochet hook, join yarn on Back Left Armhole next to shoulder seam. Working tightly, ch 1, sc in each row-end around sleeve, sl st to first sc, end off.

Note: I refrained from edging the inside shoulder as there are some holes at the edges (a natural outcome of the stitch pattern) that are accentuated when trim is worked.

Gilliam

Gilliam is a casual and comfortable sweater featuring dropped-shoulder construction worked from the bottom up. It has a wide and deep V-neck and elbow length sleeves that start out full and then taper. There's plenty of ease in the bust and bicep and ample body length.

The colorful sport weight Arroyo yarn is by Malabrigo, a company that has been at the forefront of hand-dyeing for decades. It's a great vehicle for Tunisian simple stitch, allowing the yarn itself to provide plenty of excitement. Gilliam will look lovely in a more subdued palette as well—or would you prefer to go even wilder? Luckily for today's yarnies, fabulous hand-dyed yarns come in a tremendous variety of hues and are easy to find!

FINISHED BUST MEASUREMENTS
Sizes 1 through 5.

36 (40, 44, 48, 52) in./91.5 (101.5, 112, 122, 132) cm

Suggested ease: 2–4 in./5–10 cm

MATERIALS
- Malabrigo Arroyo; 100% superwash merino; 335 yds./306 m per 3.5 oz./100 g; sport weight; Sea Horse #AR230: 3 (4, 4, 5, 5) skeins
- Suggested hook size: H-8 (5.0 mm) cabled Tunisian hook
- 2 stitch markers

GAUGE
16 sts and 15 rows = 4 in./10 cm

Gauge Swatch
Ch 24.

Work foundation row.

Row 1: Tss across, end st.

Rep Row 1 until you have a *total of* 23 rows.

Tss sl st across.

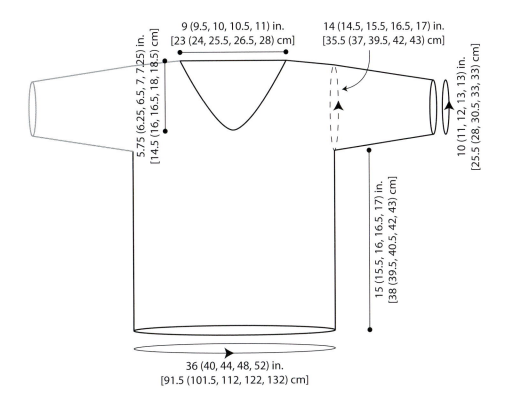

SPECIAL STITCHES AND ABBREVIATIONS

Tss2tog: Insert hook in next 2 vertical bars, draw up loop.

Dec at end of row: Work to last 3 sts, Tss2tog, end st.

Dec at beg of row: Tss2tog, cont across.

BODY

Ch 144 (160, 176, 192, 208).

Row 1: Work Basic Foundation Row.

Work Tss for a total of 56 (58, 60, 62, 64) rows, end off.

YOKE

Divide for Front and Back

Count 72 (80, 88, 96, 104) sts, PM in this st. This marks the last st of Front Yoke. The stitch after M begins the Back Yoke. Front and Back each have the same number of sts.

Back Yoke

Join yarn in st after M.

Work Tss for 27 (28, 30, 32, 33) rows, Tsl st across.

Front Yoke

Join yarn in first unworked st on Body.

Work Tss for 5 (5, 6, 6, 6) rows, placing end st in last st of row.

V-Neck Shaping

On this side, decreases are made at end of row.

Count 36 (40, 44, 48, 52) sts, PM in this st. This marks the left edge of the V-neckline (left when worn; it appears at right when viewing). There should be the same number of sts rem on Front Yoke for right side.

Next row: Tss to 3 sts before (and including) M, Tss2tog, end st in M. 35 (39, 43, 47, 51) sts

Work 14 (14, 15, 16, 16) more rows, dec at end of row, ending with 21 (25, 28, 31, 35) sts.

Next row: Work even.
Next row: Tss to 3 sts before M, Tss2tog, end st. 20 (24, 27, 30, 34) sts

Rep last 2 rows 2 (3, 3, 3, 4) more times, ending with 18 (21, 24, 27, 30) sts.

Sizes 1 and 4 Only:
Next row: Work even.

All Sizes:
Tss sl st across.

Right V-neck Shaping

On this side, decreases are made at beg of row.

Next row: Join yarn in st after M, Tss2tog, Tss across. 35 (39, 43, 47, 51) sts

Rep last row 14 (14, 15, 16, 16) more times, ending with 21 (25, 28, 31, 35) sts.

Next row: Work even.
Next row: Tss2tog, Tss across. 20 (24, 27, 30, 34) sts

Rep last 2 rows 2 (3, 3, 3, 4) more times, ending with 18 (21, 24, 27, 30) sts.

Sizes 1 and 4 Only:
Next row: Work even.

All Sizes:
Tss sl st across. Remove markers.

I recommend blocking Back, then Front, to schematic measurements before sewing side and shoulder seams and working Sleeves. Pin the Front Yoke pieces carefully so width and length dimensions on either side of V-neck match.

Sew side seam.

Work sl st seam along each shoulder. Count out stitches along top of Back, at left and right, to match stitch count at each Shoulder, and PM to indicate neck edge. With WS facing, work sl st seam, inserting hook under 2 loops on Back and 2 loops on Front. Make sure slip stitches don't tighten the fabric. When done, use a steam iron hovering above seam to relax and flatten fabric.

SLEEVES

Sleeves narrow as they get closer to elbow. Decreases are made at both beginning and end of a Forward row: in the 2nd and 3rd stitch at the start, in the 2nd and 3rd to last stitches at the end. This leaves the first and last stitch of the row undisturbed.

Join yarn in space between Front and Back at underarm, draw up loop, draw up loop in each st around sleeve, inserting hook under back loop as you work around Front and Back. 55, (57, 61, 65, 67) sts

Work 10 (12, 14, 16, 18) rows even.

Next row: Dec at beg and end of row. 53 (55, 59, 63, 65) sts

Next 2 rows: Work even.

Rep last 3 rows 6 more times, ending with 41 (43, 47, 51, 53) sts.

You should have *a total of* 31 (33, 35, 37, 39) rows.

Tsl st across.

FINISHING

Block Sleeves as needed. Sew sleeve seam.

Becca is an everyday cardigan with Front sections that are just shy of meeting at the center. It is meant to fit closely and uses a very simple dropped-shoulder construction, a good choice if you're new to garment making. The elbow-length sleeves are worked with no shaping until the cuff, where a trim of single crochet stitches tightens the bottom. The Front edges and neckline are also trimmed with single crochet stitches.

I chose Galileo sport weight, a Knit Picks yarn with some very lovely fibers—merino and bamboo viscose—that ensure drapey fabric. There is some surface texture to the yarn, which requires a stitch with strong lines, and a lovely sheen that makes everything pop.

STITCH PATTERN NOTES

This stitch pattern, similar to the one used in Aimee, features an upside-down shell. The shells alternate with a single Tss stitch. This requires a different Rtn row than the Basic Rtn row. On the Rtn row, after the initial chain and (yo, draw through 2 loops), we bring the hook through 4 loops to make the shell. We then make a chain, then bring the hook through 2 loops for the next Tss, then another chain.

Hook inserted under Rtn row

On forward rows a Tfs is worked on either side of these shells, and we also work into the chain atop the shell. For the first Tfs insert the hook under the Rtn row between a Tss and the next shell.

First Tfs made

You'll then see a small loop above the shell—insert the hook in that loop and draw up a loop.

For the second Tfs, insert the hook under the Rtn row between the shell and the next Tss and draw up a loop.

Hook inserted in loop above shell

The pattern repeat consists of the shell, which has 3 stitches, plus 1 Tss, therefore 4 stitches in total. Unlike most other stitches, there will not be a slip stitch row to end off.

To create a firm side edge for the Yoke section, which occurs after the Divide for Front and Back, increases are

Second Tfs made

68 The Tunisian Crochet Sweater Collection

made at the edges of the work. The first increase is made by drawing up a loop in the Rtn row chain at the beginning of the row, and the second increase by drawing up a loop in the Rtn row chain just before the end stitch. At the beginning of the row, be sure to make both this increase and the Tfs that follows it, to remain in pattern.

FINISHED BUST MEASUREMENTS

Sizes 1 through 6.

36.5 (40.5, 44.5, 48.5, 52.5, 56.5) in./93 (103, 113, 123, 133, 143.5) cm

Suggested ease: 2–5 in./5–13 cm

MATERIALS

- Knit Picks Galileo; 50% merino, 50% bamboo viscose; 131 yds./119.75 m per 1.75 oz./50 g; sport weight; Hesper: 7 (8, 9, 10, 12, 13) balls
- Suggested hook sizes:
  - H-8 (5.0 mm) cabled Tunisian hook
  - F-5 (3.75 mm) regular crochet hook
- 6 stitch markers

GAUGE

16 sts and 12 rows = 4 in./10 cm

Gauge Swatch

Ch 27.

Row 1 Fwd: Foundation row. **Rtn:** Yo, draw through 1 loop, *yo, draw through 2 loops, ch 1, yo, draw through 4 loops, ch 1, rep from * across, (yo, draw through 2 loops) twice. 6 Shells

Row 2 Fwd: *Tss, Tfs, draw up loop in ch atop shell, Tfs, rep from * across, Tss, end st. **Rtn:** Rep Row 1 Rtn row.

Rep Row 2 for *a total of* 20 rows.

SPECIAL STITCHES AND ABBREVIATIONS

Increase (Inc): Insert hook in next ch, draw up loop. Note that this increase occurs just before or after a Tfs. Make sure both the increase and Tfs stitches are made.

Decrease 2 sc sts (sc3tog): (Yo, insert hook in next st and draw up loop) 3 times, yo, draw through 4 loops on hook.

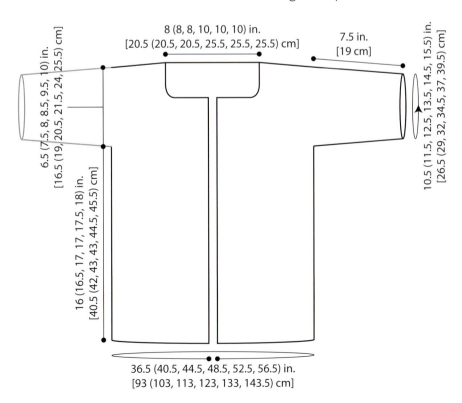

BODY

Ch 139 (155, 171, 187, 203, 219).

Row 1 Fwd: Draw up loop in each ch. **Rtn:** Yo, draw through 1 loop, *yo, draw through 2 loops, ch 1, yo, draw through 4 loops, ch 1, rep from * across, (yo, draw through 2 loops) twice. 34 (38, 42, 46, 50, 54) Shells + 2 end sts + 1 Tss.

Row 2 Fwd: *Tss, Tfs, draw up loop in ch atop shell, Tfs, rep from * across, Tss, end st. **Rtn:** Rep Row 1 Rtn row.

Rep Row 2 working a *total of* 48 (49, 50, 51, 52, 53) rows. Place working loop on holder.

YOKE

Divide for Front and Back

*Count 8 (9, 10, 11, 12, 13) shells, PM in next Tss. Beg at end of row, rep from *. You have 73 (81, 89, 97, 105, 113) sts on Back and 34 (38, 42, 46, 50, 54) on each Front. The 2 marked sts will be used on both Front and Back.

To make edges symmetrical and create firm edges for each armhole, a stitch is added at the beginning and end of the first row of the Back. The increase is made by drawing up a loop in the chain adjacent to the first and last stitches.

Back Yoke

With new ball, join yarn in 1st M, draw up loop in next ch (Inc made), work in patt to 2nd M, draw up loop in ch before M, work end st in M. 75 (83, 91, 99, 107, 115) sts, 18 (20, 22, 24, 26, 28) shells

Work a *total of* 20 (22, 24, 26, 28, 30) rows in patt, end off.

Left Front Yoke

The end of the row will not need an increase, only the beginning.

Join yarn in 2nd M, Inc, cont in patt across. 34 (38, 42, 46, 50, 54) sts, 8 (9, 10, 11, 12, 13) shells

Work 9 (10, 11, 12, 13, 14) more rows even.

Starting at end of row, count 3 (3, 3, 4, 4, 4) shells, then continue to next Tss and PM in this st.

Fwd: Work in patt to M, making last st (in M) an end st. **Rtn:** Yo, draw through 1 loop, ch 1, yo, draw through 4 loops, cont in patt across, (yo, draw through 2 loops) twice. 22 (26, 30, 30, 34, 38) sts, 5 (6, 7, 7, 8, 9) patt reps. Do not remove this M.

Work 9 (10, 11, 12, 13, 14) more rows even, always repeating last Rtn row.

You should have 20 (22, 24, 26, 28, 30) rows in total. End off.

Right Front Yoke

Pick up working loop.

Fwd: Work in patt to 2 sts before first M, Inc, end st in M. **Rtn:** Yo, draw through 1 loop, yo, draw through 2 loops, ch 1, yo, draw through 4 loops, ch 1, cont in patt across. 34 (38, 42, 46, 50, 54) sts, 8 (9, 10, 11, 12) patt reps

Work 9 (10, 11, 12, 13, 14) more rows even.

Count 3 (3, 3, 4, 4, 4) shells, then cont to next Tss and PM in this st.

Work in patt to M. Do not remove this M. 22 (26, 30, 30, 34, 38) sts, 5 (6, 7, 7, 8, 9) patt reps

Work 9 (10, 11, 12, 13, 14) more rows even.

You should have 20 (22, 24, 26, 28, 30) rows in total. End off.

Block as needed before joining shoulders.

Sew shoulder seams.

As this yarn is quite stretchy, I used a slip stitch seam to create a strong, stable shoulder seam. Hold 2 shoulder edges together with their RS facing each other. Work slip stitches across, picking up 1 or 2 loops on each side, matching stitch for stitch. It is tricky working into each chain of the return row ch, but you can skip some of them so long as you match the fans and the Tss sts on both sides and keep tension so that the fabric maintains its width.

SLEEVES

When picking up stitches for the Sleeve, we will begin and end in the same Tss st. The first stitch uses the front vertical bar of the Tss (the strand we usually work into), and the last stitch uses the back vertical bar, which sits behind the front bar.

The Sleeve is meant to end just below the elbow. Feel free to lengthen it by adding rows as needed to achieve your desired length.

Join yarn at bottom of armhole in front vertical bar of Tss and draw up loop, draw up loop in each row-end around, draw up loop in back vertical bar of same st as starting st. Work Rtn row in patt. 42 (46, 50, 54, 58, 62) sts

Work a *total of* 22 rows, place loop on holder.

Try on sleeve to see if additional rows are needed. You can use safety pins along sleeve seam to hold sleeve to arm. If additional length is needed, work even until reaching desired length.

Sew sleeve seam.

Sleeve Cuff

Pick up working loop with regular crochet hook.

Ch 1, *sc in ch of Rtn row, sc in next Tss, sc in next ch of Rtn row, sc in top of Shell, rep from * around sleeve, sl st to first st. Do not turn.

Next row: Ch 1, sc in each sc around, sl st to first sc, do not turn.

Rep last row 3 more times, end off.

FINISHING

Center Front and Neckline Trim

Six markers are needed to indicate placement of shaping around and into corners. There are already 2 markers placed earlier at edges where the neckline meets the shoulder. On garment left and right, PM in each corner where the center Front meets the neckline. PM in corner sts where Front shoulders meet Back neck.

Where the Fronts meet the neckline we make increases; at other markers we make decreases. Move markers up either to the center stitch of increase or into the top of the sc3tog, as appropriate.

With regular crochet hook, join yarn at bottom right hem (left for left-handers), sc in each row-end along front, work 3 sc in first M, *sc in ch of Rtn row, sc in next Tss, sc in next ch of Rtn row, sc in top of Shell, rep from * to 1 st before next M, sc3tog, sc in each row-end along shoulder, sc across back in same manner as on Front neckline, sc in each row-end along 2nd shoulder to 1 st before next M, sc3tog, continue working across opposite Front neckline, 3 sc in last M, continue to bottom, turn. Move up all M.

Next row: Ch 1, sc in each sc to M, 3 sc in M, *sc in each sc to 1 st before M, sc3tog, rep from * 3 times, sc in each sc to last M, sc3tog, sc in each st across.

Rep last row 1 (1, 1, 2, 2, 2) times.

If you would like to have the Fronts meet at center, feel free to add a few more rows of trim.

Block Sleeves as needed.

Lightweight and clingy, this little lace top can go from dinner to club with aplomb.

The construction is dropped shoulder, worked from the bottom in one piece up to the armhole, then divided in half for Front and Back Yoke. The Front Yoke has a square dropped neckline that requires no shaping. In other words, this is quite an easy pattern, but the stitch may require a bit of practice. It's a beauty though, so well worth the effort.

I've long admired the yarns made by the Turkish company Urth Yarns, as they feature high-quality fibers like this extrafine merino (super soft and pliable) and offer a fine selection of colors. Spiral Grain is a very interesting yarn that changes color gradually, almost imperceptibly, and then all of a sudden you have a different color on the hook.

STITCH PATTERN NOTES

What's unusual about this stitch pattern is that there are double the number of chains in the return row than there are stitches in the forward row. That's because there is a chain between each forward row stitch. The forward row strands stretch out so that they match the return row in length. The result is fabric with a lovely, built-in stretchiness that will make this design accommodate many sizes. For purposes of counting stitches, we will always use the forward row.

Forward Row

The stitch pattern consists of two stitches: Tps and Tdc2tog, alternating the order in each row. Tdc2tog is very similar to what we do when working regular crochet dc2tog. At the top of the Tdc2tog is a vertical bar where you will insert your hook when working a Tps on the following row.

Return Row with 2 chains between each stitch

It can be hard to identify the last stitch—the end stitch—of the forward row, because it's right next to two chains. If needed, PM in end stitch right after making it, and move M up each row.

Layla

FINISHED BUST MEASUREMENTS

Sizes 1 through 5.

35 (39, 44, 48, 52) in./89 (99, 112, 122, 132) cm

Suggested ease: negative 1–3 in./2.5–7.5 cm

MATERIALS

- Urth Yarns Spiral Grain; 100% extrafine merino; 198 yds./180 m per 1.75 oz./50 g; sport weight; Sugar Pine: (4, 4, 5, 6) skeins
- Suggested hook size: H-8 (5.0 mm) cabled Tunisian hook
- 2 stitch markers

GAUGE

11 sts and 9 rows = 4 in./10 cm

Gauge Swatch

Ch 33.

Row 1 Fwd: *Sk next ch, Tdc2tog in next ch, sk next ch, draw up loop in next ch, rep from * across. **Rtn:** Yo, draw through 1 loop, *ch 1, yo, draw through 2 loops, rep from * across, end st. 17 sts

Rep Row 1 until you have a *total* of 14 rows.

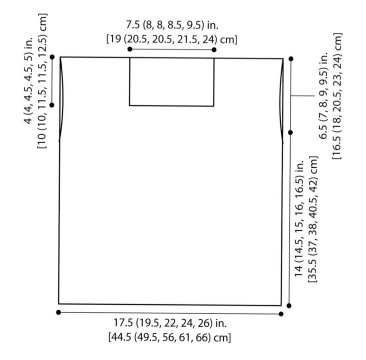

SPECIAL STITCH AND ABBREVIATION

Work 2 Tunisian double crochet stitches together (Tdc2tog): (Yo, insert hook in next bar and draw up loop, yo, draw through 2 loops) twice, yo, draw through 2 loops. Note that the hook is inserted in **same** st twice.

BODY

Ch 191 (215, 239, 263, 287).

Row 1 Fwd: Do not work regular foundation row. *Sk next ch, Tdc2tog in next ch, sk next ch, draw up loop in next ch, rep from * across. **Rtn:** Yo, draw through 1 loop, *ch 1, yo, draw through 2 loops, rep from * across. 96 (108, 120, 132, 144) sts

Row 2: *Tps in Tdc2tog**, Tdc2tog in Tps, rep from * ending last rep at **, end st.

Work in patt completing a *total* of 31 (33, 34, 36, 37) rows.

YOKE

Divide for Front and Back

Count 48 (54, 60, 66, 72) sts. PM in this st. This is the last st of the Back. The Front Yoke will begin in the next st after M.

Back Yoke

Work in patt to M, placing end st in M.

Cont in patt working a *total* of 15 (16, 18, 20, 21) rows.

Last row end-off: This end-off row is designed to keep the last row the same width as earlier rows. For this reason, we work Tunisian slip stitch row using the number of stitches in the Fwd row. The slip stitches should be worked rather loosely—use your eye to check that fabric is staying even. This method makes the shoulder a bit narrower, with less fabric dropping down onto the upper arm.

If row begins with Tps work as follows: Tsl st in next st, Tps sl st in next st, rep from * across, end off.

If row begins with Tdc2tog work: Tps sl st in next, Tsl st in next st, rep from across, end off.

76 The Tunisian Crochet Sweater Collection

Front Yoke

Join yarn 1 st after M. Then remove this M.

Work in patt for 6 (7, 8, 10, 10) rows.

First Shoulder

* Count 14 (16, 19, 21, 23) sts and PM. Beg at end of row rep from *. This leaves 20 (22, 22, 24, 26) sts between M for the front neck.

Work in patt to M, placing end st in M.

Work a *total* of 9 (9, 10, 10, 11) rows.

Work last row end-off (see Back Yoke).

Second Shoulder

You will not need very much yarn for this second Front Shoulder, though the amount varies by size, of course. Think about the following: If you are using a self-striping yarn, you want your two Front sections to be somewhat alike. See what's left on any partial balls you have used in this project. Find one that allows you to start with a color that's similar to where you left off on Front. From there, the two Shoulders will vary, of course, but this will help harmonize.

Before beginning the 2nd shoulder we will end off the stitches on the neckline between shoulders.

Join yarn in last st of first row of shoulder. Work last row end-off to next M (see Back Yoke).

Now continue on same row working in patt across.

Work a *total* of 9 (9, 10, 10, 11) rows in patt.

Work last row end-off.

FINISHING

Wet block to desired measurements. You may wish to block the Front and Back separately.

Sew side seam from garment bottom to underarm.

Shoulder seams can be either sewn or done with slip stitches from WS.

Joni

This cute tee features the ever popular and attractive honeycomb stitch. It is designed for a relaxed fit with length to high hip. Joni is worked top down with raglan increases. Once you've finished the yoke, the sleeves are done, too, except for trim. This is a good choice for your first garment worked top down. Be sure to read all the previous pages on raglan shaping, placing markers, counting stitches, and so on.

For this short-sleeved garment, I sought a pliable cotton and found it in Jody Long worsted weight yarn. Jody is a very talented Australian knitting designer who has developed his own line of yarns, and he clearly understands that worsted weight needs to be super soft to function well for garments. This one really does, and it feels awesome on the skin as well. I refrained from blocking, however, as soft cotton can stretch quite a bit when wet.

FINISHED BUST MEASUREMENTS

Sizes 1 through 5.

35 (38.5, 43, 47.5, 51) in./89 (98, 109, 120.5, 129.5) cm

Suggested ease: 1–3 in./2.5–7.5 cm

MATERIALS

- Jody Long Cottontails; 100% cotton; 164 yds./150 m per 2.5 oz./75 g; light worsted weight; Sky #018: 3 (4, 5, 5, 6) balls, Candy #021: 1 (1, 1, 1, 2) ball(s) (for trim)
- Suggested hook sizes:
  - K-10½ (6.5 mm) cabled Tunisian hook
  - J-10 (6.0 mm) cabled Tunisian hook
- 4 stitch markers

GAUGE

14 sts and 12 rows in honeycomb st = 4 in./10 cm

Honeycomb Stitch Gauge Swatch

Ch 22.

Work foundation row.

Row 1: *Tss in next st, Tps in next st, rep from * across.

Row 2: *Tps in Tss, Tss in Tps, rep from * across.

Rep Rows 1 and 2 until you have *a total of* 18 rows.

Tps being made

Tss being made

SPECIAL STITCH AND ABBREVIATION

Increase (Inc): Draw up loop in ch before M, Tks in M, draw up loop in next ch.

Loop drawn up in chain before marker for raglan increase

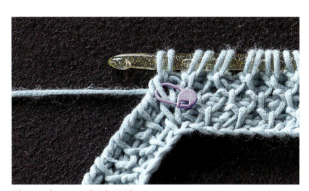

Tks made in marked stitch

Loop drawn up in chain after marker for raglan increase

Joni **81**

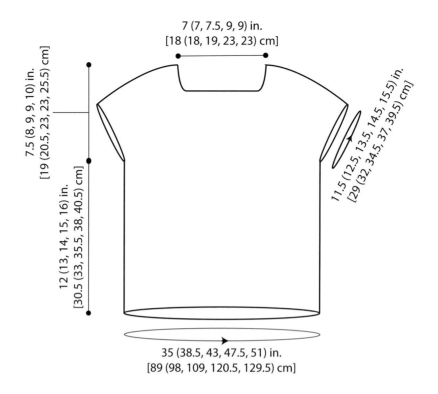

NOTE

The pattern will omit instructions for last stitch. You can either use the traditional end stitch and sew the back seam when finishing, or use the connecting stitch and join as you go. If you decide on the latter, wait until you have completed at least three rows before using it, as it can be very difficult to keep work from twisting until you have more fabric. You can sew these few rows together when finishing.

YOKE

With larger hook, ch 92 (92, 100, 108, 108) sts.

Row 1: Work Basic Foundation Row.

Place markers for raglan stitches:

From beginning of row, count 12 (12, 14, 16, 16) sts, PM in next st. Beginning in next st, count 19 (19, 21, 21, 21) sts and PM in next st. Now, starting at opposite end of the row, count 13 (13, 13, 15, 15) sts and PM in next st. Beginning in next st, count 19 (19, 21, 21, 21) sts and PM in next st. You have placed 4M, which are the raglan stitches.

You should have 25 (25, 27, 31, 31) sts on the Front/Back (Back sections are at beginning and end) and 19 (19, 21, 21, 21) sts on each Sleeve.

Row 2: Tss in next st, Tps in next st, cont in Honeycomb patt to first M, Inc, *Tss in next st, cont in Honeycomb patt** to next M, Inc, rep from * 4 times ending last rep at **. 100 (100, 108, 116, 116) sts. Front/Back sts: 27 (27, 29, 33, 33). Sleeve sts: 21 (21, 23, 23, 23) sts

Move all M up to st worked into M.

Row 3: *Tps in next st, Tss in next st, cont in patt** to M, Inc, Tss in next st, rep from * 4 times ending last rep at **. 108 (108, 116, 124, 124) sts. Front/Back sts: 29 (29, 31, 35, 35), Sleeve sts: 23 (23, 25, 25, 25)

Rows 4–7 (8, 8, 8, 9): Rep Rows 2 and 3 (*some sizes will end with Row 2*), adding 8 sts on each row, ending with 140 (148, 156, 164, 172) sts. Front/Back sts: 37 (39, 41, 45, 47). Sleeve sts: 31 (33, 35, 35, 37)

From this point, there will be no further increases on Sleeves. Sleeve counts remain the same as previous row till end of yoke.

Row 8 (9, 9, 9, 10): Work in patt to next M, *draw up loop in ch before M, Tks in M, do not work Inc after M, Tss in next st, cont in patt to next M, do not Inc before M, Tks in M, draw up loop in ch after M, Tss in next st, cont in patt to next M, rep from * once and work in patt to end. 144 (152, 160, 168, 176) sts. Front/Back sts: 39 (41, 43, 47, 49)

Row 9 (10, 10, 10, 11): Work in patt to next M, draw up loop in ch before M, Tks in M, do not work Inc after M, Tps in next st, cont in patt to next M, do not Inc before M, Tks in M, draw up loop in ch after M, Tps in next st, cont in patt to next M, draw up loop in ch before M, Tks in M, do not work Inc after M, Tps in next st, cont in patt to next M, do not Inc before next M, Tks in M, draw up loop in ch after M, Tss in next st, work in patt across. 148 (156, 164, 172, 180) sts. Front/Back sts 41 (43, 45, 49, 51).

Rows 10–14 (11–17, 11–19, 11–19, 12–21): Continue in patt rep prev 2 rows. 168 (180, 196, 204, 216) sts. Front/Back sts: 51 (57, 63, 67, 71). Sleeve sts: 31 (33, 35, 35, 37)

Sizes 2, 3, and 4 only:
Continue to Body.

Sizes 1 and 5 only:
Row 15 (22 and 23): Work in pattern without increases. Continue to Body.

BODY

Place working loop on holder. With separate strand, join yarn in first M, ch 8 (8, 10, 14, 16), sl st to 2nd M, end off. With separate strand, join yarn in 3rd M, ch 8 (8, 10, 14, 16), sl st to 4th M, end off. Do not remove M yet.

Note: M is a Tks and has 2 separate strands, 1 on right and 1 on left. On first row of Body, use the strand at right. Use strand at left for when beginning sleeve. (Left-handers, reverse all instructions.) The Body will gain 4 sts.

Row 1: *Work in patt across to M, draw up loop in each ch, Tps in next M, cont in patt across to next M, rep from * across. 122 (134, 150, 166, 178) sts. Remove M.

PM in center st at each underarm. We will use these M to begin Sleeve trim.

Work in patt till length from underarm measures 12 (13, 14, 15, 16) in./30.5 (33, 35.5, 38, 41) cm or desired length. Feel free to adjust this length to whatever your preference is, keeping in mind that this may affect the amount of yarn used. The Trim at bottom will add approx. 1 in./2.5 cm of length.

FINISHING

Sew back seam.

The dimensions on schematic do not take Trim into account. Neckline will be approx. 3 in./7.5 cm smaller after Trim, and each Sleeve opening will also be approx. 3 in./7.5 cm smaller. Hem circumference will lose a few inches as well. This schematic allows you to measure your garment before adding Trim.

I recommend trying on garment before working Trim. See Blocking section below. Then, depending on how it fits at the hem, sleeve edges, and neckline, you can make each part more snug or keep it as is. For the former, use a smaller hook as per instructions. For the latter, use the same size hook.

Neckline Trim

With Trim yarn and one size smaller hook, join yarn at seam on back neck.

Row 1: Draw up a loop in each base ch around, end st, work Rtn row. 92 (92, 100, 108, 108) sts

Rows 2 and 3: Tks across, end st.

Row 4: Tss sl st across, end st. End off.

Sew up trim at back neck.

Hem Trim

Join Trim yarn at center back seam. Follow instructions for Rows 1–4 of Neckline Trim.

Sleeve Trim

The sleeve will gain an additional 8 (8, 10, 14, 16) sts added at underarm plus 2 raglan sts. You should have the following number of sts on sleeve: 41 (43, 47, 51, 55) sts. If you are off by just a couple, it's fine.

Row 1: Join yarn at marked center st at underarm. Draw up loop in each st at underarm and in each st around.

Rows 2–4: Follow instructions for Rows 2–4 of Neckline Trim.

Blocking

I did not wet block the entire sweater, as cotton can stretch out of shape. Whether or not to block your version depends on the yarn you've chosen. Either way, the Trim will need wet blocking to lie flat. To block Trim only, try this method: With water spritzer, wet Trim only at neck, hem, and armhole, pin on blocking board and let dry.

Kelcy

This cardigan is meant to be both casual and classy, with a fairly open neck and an easygoing, loose fit. It features a ribbed stitch made with Tks and Tps stitches that yields a fluid, comfortable-to-wear fabric. The raglan line consists of 4 Tks stitches, to make it pop from the surrounding texture. The button band is worked in Tks. Sleeves are worked without shaping, so they are full, then cuffed at the bottom.

For this design I chose a beautiful DK weight yarn by Knit Picks called Capra, notable for its fabulous fibers: merino with a touch of cashmere. Nothing drapes as nicely, and there's lovely sheen too. And of course, it will keep you toasty when needed!

STITCH AND PATTERN NOTES

When working this stitch pattern, keep in mind that Tks is a tight stitch by nature and therefore requires a loose hand to yield a wearable fabric. Work loosely throughout. The purl stitches are naturally larger, and that's OK. Resist the urge to tighten up your stitches, whether knit or purl, as you work. They may look large, but once worked into in the next row, they will be the right size.

This stitch pattern consists of 3 sts: 2 Tks, Tps.

When instructions say to remain in pattern, repeat these three stitches. Keep in mind that the stitches always align from row to row, that is, Tps will always be worked into Tps, Tks into Tks. Where increases occur, work in pattern over newly added stitches, as spelled out in instructions. You will see the ribbed look after a few rows.

For a decorative effect along the raglan line, four Tks stitches are used. Increases will be made on each side of these four raglan stitches. All increases are made by drawing up a loop in the Rtn row chain. Once the yoke is done, the raglan stitches will be incorporated into the pattern.

Inserting for Tks

2 Tks made

Bring yarn forward for Tps

Note that except for Front sections, each section begins and ends with the same stitch. For example, in Row 2, each section begins and ends with Tps. In Rows 3 and 4, they begin and end with Tks. We are adding stitches in pattern at each end of each section as we make the Yoke. At a later point in the pattern, this will no longer apply, as we stop increasing on the Sleeves but not on the Body. By the end of the yoke, all sections will have Tps on either side of raglan stitches.

Be very attentive as you work each raglan increase. The stitches can be tricky to read, especially the increase right after the 4 Tks, because stitches will tend to bunch together. Work slowly and make sure you are placing the increase stitch correctly, in the space between the last Tks and the following increase stitch.

FINISHED BUST MEASUREMENTS

Sizes 1 through 5.

35 (40.5, 44, 48, 52.5) in./89 (103, 112, 122, 133.5) cm

Suggested ease: 1–4 in./2.5–10 cm

MATERIALS

- Knit Picks Capra; 85% merino, 15% cashmere; 123 yds./112.5 m per 1.75 oz./50 g; DK weight; Ciel: 10 (13, 16, 18, 22) balls
- Suggested hook sizes:
  - J-10 (6.0 mm) cabled Tunisian hook
  - I-9 (5.5 mm) cabled Tunisian hook (for sleeve cuff only)
- 7 (7, 7, 8, 8) buttons, 1 in./2.5 cm diameter
- 7 or 8 stitch markers (for raglans and for buttons)

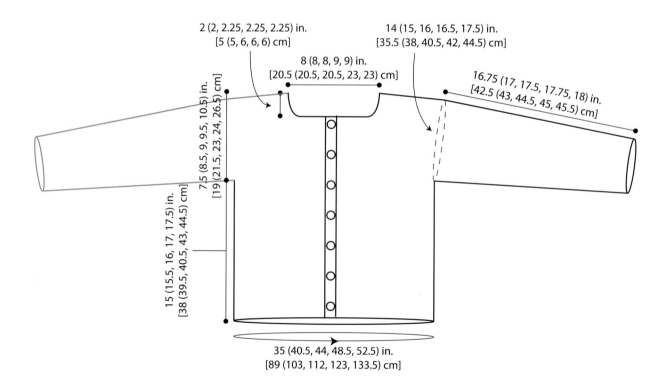

GAUGE

4 patt repeats (12 sts) = 3.5 in./9 cm; 10 rows = 3 in./7.5 cm

Gauge Swatch

Ch 26.

Work foundation row.

Row 1: Tps, * 2 Tks, Tps; rep from * across, end st.

Rep Row 1 until you have *a total of* 23 rows.

SPECIAL STITCH AND ABBREVIATIONS

Increase (Inc): Insert hook in next rtn row ch and draw up loop.

Tks decrease (Tks2tog): Insert hook in front vertical bar of next st (as in Tss), then insert hook in following st as in Tks, draw up loop.

YOKE

Ch 77 (77, 83, 92, 92).

Row 1: Work Basic Foundation Row.

*Count 8 (8, 8, 11, 11) sts and PM in next st (for left Front). Beg in next st, count 3 sts and PM in next st (for raglan sts). Beg in next st, count 13 (13, 16, 16, 16) sts and PM in next st (for left Sleeve).

Beg at end of row rep from * to place M for right Front, raglan sts, and right Sleeve. You will have 8 (8, 8, 11, 11) sts on each Front, 13 (13, 16, 16, 16) sts on each Sleeve, 19 (19, 19, 22, 22) sts on Back, and 16 raglan sts.

Row 2: *Tps, 2 Tks, cont in patt placing Tps in st before M, Inc, Tks in M and next 3 sts, Inc, rep from * across, cont in patt placing last Tps before end st. (85, 85, 91, 100, 100) sts.

Kelcy 89

Row 3: Tps, 2 Tks, *cont in patt placing Tks in st before M, Inc, 4 Tks, Inc, Tks, Tps, 2 Tks, rep from * across, cont in patt placing last Tps before end st. 93 (93, 99, 108, 108) sts.

Row 4: Tps, 2 Tks *cont in patt placing Tks in st before M, Inc, 4 Tks, Inc, 2 Tks, Tps, rep from * across, end st. 101 (101, 107, 116, 116) sts.

Next 9 Rows: Rep Rows 2–4 three more times. 173 (173, 179, 188, 188) sts. You will have 20 (20, 20, 23, 23) sts on each Front, 37 (37, 40, 40, 40) sts on each Sleeve, 43 (43, 43, 46, 46) on Back, and 16 raglan sts.

There will be no further increases for Sleeves, only for Fronts and Back. Four stitches are added per row. Remove the 2nd, 3rd, 6th, and 7th markers to signal no increase. From this point Sleeve sections will begin and end with a Tps next to the raglan st, while the Fronts and Back continue to add stitches in pattern.

Next 3 (6, 9, 9, 12) rows: Work in patt Inc at each M. 185 (197, 215, 224, 236) sts. 23 (26, 29, 32, 35) sts on each Front, 37 (37, 40, 40, 40) sts on each Sleeve, 49 (55, 61, 64, 70) sts on Back, and 16 raglan sts.

Work even for 3 (2, 0, 2, 1) rows.

You should have a *total of* 19 (21, 22, 24, 26) rows in Yoke.

BODY

Move each M to space between 2nd and 3rd Tks of raglan line. With separate strand, join yarn in first M, ch 7 (10, 10, 13, 16), sl st to 2nd M, end off. With separate strand, join yarn in 3rd M, ch 7 (10, 10, 13, 16), sl st to 4th M, end off.

Row 1: (Work in patt to underarm chains, draw up a loop in each ch) twice, cont in patt across. 117 (135, 147, 162, 180) sts

Row 2: [Work in patt to underarm sts, (Tps, 2 Tks) 2 (3, 3, 4, 5) times, Tps] twice, cont in patt across.

Work even in patt completing a *total of* 50 (52, 54, 56, 58) rows. Remove all M.

To avoid curl at the bottom edge, an X-st is used for the last slip stitch row:

Last row: Tsl st across in X-st patt, that is, sk next st, draw up loop in next st and through loop on hook, draw up loop in skipped st and through loop on hook.

SLEEVES

Sleeve is worked even, then gathered at the bottom by skipping all Tps, as indicated in instructions. You will then have Tks sts only. You can make the sleeve to your preferred length—all the way to the wrist or perhaps just below the elbow—your choice, easily determined by trying the garment on.

Row 1: Join yarn in base ch of 4th (4th, 4th, 7th, 7th) st at underarm; draw up a loop in each ch, work in patt around Sleeve, draw up a loop in each rem chains at underarm. 48 (51, 54, 57, 60) sts

Row 2: 2 Tks, Tps, cont in patt across, end st.

Work even in patt for a *total of* 53 (54, 55, 56, 57) rows.

Next row: With smaller hook, *2 Tks, sk Tps, rep from * across, end st. 32 (34, 36, 38, 40) sts

Next 2 rows: Tks2tog, Tks across to last 3 sts, Tks2tog, end st. 28 (30, 32, 34, 36) sts

Work Tss sl st across. Do not use Tks sl st.

You should have a *total of* 56 (57, 58, 59, 60) rows on Sleeve.

FINISHING
Left Button Band
Join yarn on left-hand side of Front at top of garment. Work into 2 loops at the side edge.

Row 1: Inserting hook under both loops, draw up a loop in each st to garment bottom, work Rtn row.
Rows 2–4: Tks across. Tss sl st across.
Place markers for buttons: The aim is to sew buttons nicely centered on band. PM in center of band as follows: 3rd st from top, *count 9 sts and PM in center of band, rep from * to bottom, leaving 4–10 sts with no button. When working buttonholes, we have to match this bottom button, so count how many rows are below it.

Right Buttonhole Band
This side has buttonholes worked in Row 2.

Join yarn at right-hand side of Front at bottom. Rep Row 1 of left side.

Place markers for buttonholes: PM in each row that aligns with markers on opposite side—you can count sts from the top beginning in 3rd st and marking every 9th st from there; be sure to have the same number of rows below the bottom button.

Row 2: *Tks to marked st, yo, sk next st, rep from * across, Tks to end.
Row 3: *Tks to yo, draw up loop in yo (visible as a slanted line across the return row), rep from * across, Tks to end.
Row 4: Tks across. Tss sl st across.

Blocking
You may wish to block this in sections. Be sure to pin the neckline and bottom liberally to eliminate curl. Sew buttons in place after blocking.

Vanessa and Tess are a two-piece set that can fit into your wardrobe in so many ways! The sweater has a fairly close neckline, a comfortable and flattering fit, and elbow-length sleeves. The pattern can be worked with a connecting stitch at the ends of rows or the usual end stitch with seam at center back.

Hobbii is a fairly recent addition to the yarn scene that is attracting many crafters to its affordable and versatile yarns. Happy Place was created by the outstanding designer Toni Lipsey, a specialist in Tunisian crochet. It's a DK weight that combines cotton and wool and comes in many attractive colors, both solid and subtly flecked. To bring out the best in this yarn, I chose a three-stitch pattern that combines a Tps and an X stitch (the latter requires two stitches). The Tps lends drape, and the X stitch adds a strong visual element and stitch definition to the flecked color.

Skip next st, Tss in next st

X-stitch worked

There is a ribbed look to this stitch pattern that I find appealing, and it has some of the stretchiness of ribbing too. Against this background, the raglan line for this design consists of three Tss stitches. Raglan increases are made before and after this three-stitch group by drawing up a loop in the return row chain just before the first Tss of the group and just after the third Tss of the group. Keep your marker in the center Tss of the group.

Tps after X-stitch

FINISHED BUST MEASUREMENTS

Sizes 1 through 5.

34.5 (37.5, 42, 46.5, 51) in./87.5 (95.5, 106.5, 118, 129.5) cm

Suggested ease: 0–3in./0–7.5 cm

MATERIALS

- Hobbii Happy Place Melange; 50% cotton, 50% wool; 273 yds./249.5 m per 3.5 oz./100 g; DK weight; Aubergine: 4 (5, 5, 6, 6) balls
- Suggested hook size: H-8 (5.0 mm) cabled Tunisian hook
- 4 stitch markers

GAUGE

4 patt reps (12 sts) and 10 rows = 3 in./7.5 cm

Gauge Swatch

Ch 39.

Row 1: Basic foundation row.
Row 2: *Tps, X-st, rep from * across, Tps, end st.

Rep Row 2 until you have *a total of* 20 rows.

Last row: Tps sl st, sk next st, Tss sl st in next st, Tss sl st in sk st, rep from * across.

SPECIAL STITCHES AND ABBREVIATIONS

X-stitch (X): Sk next st, Tss in next st, Tss in sk st.

Increase (Inc): Insert hook in next return row ch and draw up loop.

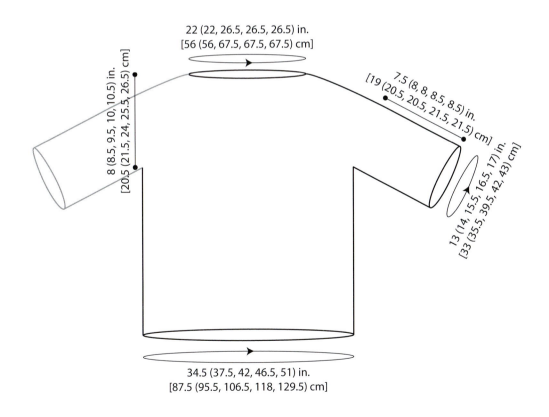

YOKE

Ch 88 (88, 106, 106, 106).

Row 1: Work Basic Foundation Row.

*Count 14 (14, 17, 17, 17) sts, PM in next st. Count 12 (12, 15, 15, 15) sts, PM in next st. Beg at end of row, rep from *.

Row 2: *(Tps, X) to M, 3 Tss, rep from * 3 more times, (Tps, X) to last 2 sts, Tps, end st.

You should have 14 (14, 17, 17, 17) sts on each half Back, 10 (10, 13, 13, 13) on each Sleeve, 28 (28, 34, 34, 34) sts on Front, and 12 raglan sts. Move M up to center Tss of raglan line each row.

Row 3: *(Tps, X) to 1 st before M, Inc, 3 Tss, Inc, rep from * 3 more times, (Tps, X) to last 2 sts, Tps, end st. 96 (96, 114, 114, 114) sts. Front/Back sts: 30 (30, 36, 36, 36); Sleeve sts: 12 (12, 15, 15, 15)

Row 4: *Work in patt to 1 st before M, Tss, Inc, 3 Tss, Inc, Tss (counts as 1 st of X), rep from * 3 more times, cont in patt, Tps, end st. 104 (104, 122, 122, 122). Front/Back sts: 32 (32, 38, 38, 38); Sleeve sts 14 (14, 17, 17, 17)

Row 5: *Work in patt to 2 sts before M, X, Inc, 3 Tss, Inc, X, rep from * 3 more times, cont in patt, Tps, end st. 112 (112, 130, 130, 130) sts. Front/Back sts: 34 (34, 40, 40, 40); Sleeve sts: 16 (16, 19, 19, 19)

Rows 6–14 (6–17, 6–17, 6–17, 6–17): Rep Rows 3–5 3 (4, 4, 4, 4) times 184 (208, 226, 226, 226) sts. Front/Back sts: 52 (58, 64, 64, 64); Sleeve sts: 36 (42, 45, 45, 45)

Row 15 (18, 18, 18, 18): Work in patt with no increases.

Row 16 (19, 19, 19, 19, 19): Rep Row 3. 192 (216, 234, 234, 234) sts. Front/Back sts: 54 (60, 66, 66, 66); Sleeve sts: 36 (42, 45, 45, 45).

Row 17 (20, 20, 20, 20): Work in patt with no increases.

Row 18 (21, 21, 21, 21): Rep Row 4. 200 (224, 242, 242, 242) sts. Front/Back sts: 56 (62, 68, 68, 68); Sleeve sts: 38, 44, 47, 47, 47).

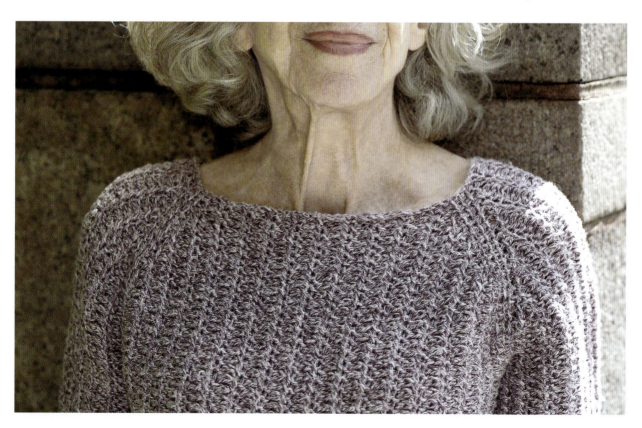

Row 19 (22, 22, 22, 22): Work in patt with no increases.

Row 20 (23, 23, 23, 23): Rep Row 5. 208 (232, 250, 250, 250) sts. Front/Back sts: 58 (64, 70); Sleeve sts: 40 (46, 49).

There will be no further increases on Sleeve. Continue increasing in patt on Body.

Sizes 1, 2, and 3 Only:
Rows 21 and 22 (24, 24–26): Work even.

Sizes 4 and 5 Only:
Rows 24–26 (24–29): *Work in patt to 1 st before 1st M, Inc, 3 Tss, cont in patt to next M, do not increase, 3 Tss, Inc, rep from *, cont in patt, end st. 262 (274) sts. Front/Back, 76 (82) sts; Sleeve, 49 (49) sts.

Size 5 Only:
Work one row even.

You should have *a total of* 22, 24, 26, 27, 29 rows on Yoke. Place working loop on holder.

BODY

All M should now be in the center st of the 3 Tss of raglan line. With separate strand, join yarn in first M, ch 7 (7, 10, 13, 16), sl st to 2nd M, end off. With separate strand, join yarn in 3rd M, ch 7 (7, 10, 13, 16), sl st to 4th M, end off.

In the first row of the Body, we convert raglan stitches into X-sts. This occurs just before and after the underarm chains. We use two out of the three raglan sts, leaving the third one for the Sleeve. The center raglan st will be used on both Body and Sleeve. Keep M in place for reference when beginning Sleeve.

Row 1: *Work in patt to first Tss, sk next st, Tss in next st, Tss in sk st (X-st made), draw up loop in each underarm ch, sk next st, Tss in next st, Tss in sk st (X-st made), rep from *, cont in patt across, end st. 138 (150, 168, 186, 204) sts

Row 2: *Work in patt to underarm sts, (Tps, X-st) 2 (2, 3, 4, 5) times, rep from *, cont in patt across, end st

Rep Row 2 for a *total of* 46 (48, 50, 52, 54) rows.

Last row: *Tps sl st, sk next st, Tss sl st in next st, Tss sl st in sk st, rep from * across, end st.

SLEEVES

Note that sleeves are not precisely symmetrical at edges, due to the odd number of stitches. For this reason, decreases are slightly different at beg and end of row, as indicated below.

Row 1: Draw up loop in base ch of center st at underarm. This should align with a Tps st. Draw up loop in next 3 (3, 4, 6, 7) base ch, X over next 2 sts (formerly 2 raglan sts), cont in patt across to 2 sts before underarm ch (formerly 2 raglan sts), X-st, draw up loop in next 3 (3, 5, 6, 8) base ch at underarm. 51 (57, 63, 66, 69) sts

Row 2: X, Tps, cont in patt across to last 2 sts, Tss, end st.

Rep Row 2, working a *total of* 25 (26, 27, 28, 29) rows.

Cuff

Next row: *Sk Tps, X, rep from * across. 34, (38, 42, 44, 46) sts

Rep last row 2 more times.

Tsl st across in X-st patt, that is, sk next st, draw up loop in next st and through loop on hook, draw up loop in skipped st and through loop on hook. This will give a better finish than pattern st, so do not work any Tps sl sts.

FINISHING

Block as needed. Sew sleeve seams.

Tess is a short skirt that is worked top down, starting just below the waist, worked flat, and seamed at center back. It uses the same rib-like stitch featured in Vanessa. After completing the body of the skirt, a Tss trim is worked along the top edge to remove approximately 3 in./7.5 cm for a closer fit at the waist. This is adjustable depending on how much slimmer you wish it to be.

To shape the skirt, markers are evenly placed around the Body and increases are made, at first on both sides of the marker, to add eight stitches per increase row, then on one side of the marker only, adding four stitches per row. This is how the gradual increase from waist to hip is accomplished. Once all increases are completed, the marked stitches can easily be incorporated into pattern. From that point, the skirt is worked even until it measures your desired length.

The natural stretch in this stitch pattern will create approximately 2 in./5 cm of ease in the garment when worn. Pick your size based on your actual hip measurement plus 0–3 in./0–7.5 cm of ease.

If you'd like your skirt fuller in the hips, work increases on both sides of the marker throughout. This will add 3 in./7.5 cm of circumference to the skirt. Your stitch count will go up by eight on every row. Keep in mind that in order to stay in pattern, the marker must have an X-st on each side when you end the increases. This way, once your desired circumference is reached, the marked stitch can be worked as a Tps and will be in pattern for the remainder of the skirt.

To make the waist smaller, work another row at the waistband to make additional decreases, as was done in the previous row.

The waist is secured with buttons and snaps. We make small flaps at the center back on each side to accommodate buttons and buttonholes. Below that flap, the two edges are sewn together to about 4 in./10 cm from the hem, which is left open so that one can walk and move easily in the skirt.

FINISHED HIP MEASUREMENTS

36 (40, 45, 50, 55) in./91.5 (101.5, 114.5, 127, 139.5) cm

MATERIALS

- Hobbii Happy Place Melange; 50% cotton, 50% wool; 273 yds./250 m per 3.5 oz./100 g; DK weight; Aubergine: 3 (3, 4, 4, 5) balls
- Suggested hook size: H-8 (5.0 mm) cabled Tunisian hook
- 4 stitch markers
- 3 shanked buttons, approx. ½ in./1 cm in diameter
- 4 small sew-on snaps

GAUGE

12 sts and 10 rows in patt = 3 in./7.5 cm

For Tss waistband only: 11 sts = 3 in./7.5 cm

Gauge Swatch

Ch 39.

Row 1: Basic foundation row.
Row 2: *Tps, X, rep from * across, Tps, end st.

Rep Row 2 until you have *a total of* 20 rows.
Last row: *Tps sl st, sk next st, Tss sl st in next st, Tss sl st in skipped st, rep from * across.

NOTES

When we begin, each section between markers begins and ends with the same stitch, and stitches are added in pattern at both edges when increasing. When increasing happens on only one side of the marker, the stitches before and after it will be different. By the end of the last increase, the stitches on either side of the marker are the same again, and they are X-sts. When the Body continues after all increases are made, the marked stitch becomes a Tps to integrate into the stitch pattern.

SPECIAL STITCHES AND ABBREVIATIONS

X-stitch (X): Sk next st, Tss in next st, Tss in sk st.

Increase (Inc): Draw up loop in ch.

Tss decrease (Tss2tog): Insert hook in next 2 vertical bars, draw up loop.

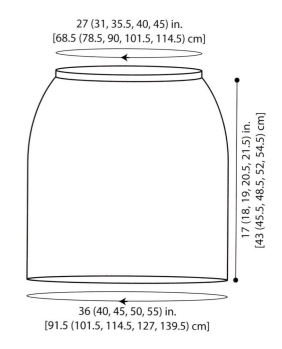

27 (31, 35.5, 40, 45) in.
[68.5 (78.5, 90, 101.5, 114.5) cm]

17 (18, 19, 20.5, 21.5) in.
[43 (45.5, 48.5, 52, 54.5) cm]

36 (40, 45, 50, 55) in.
[91.5 (101.5, 114.5, 127, 139.5) cm]

SKIRT

Ch 116 (132, 152, 172, 192).

Row 1: Work Basic Foundation Row.

Count 15 (17, 19, 22, 24) sts, PM in this st, [beg in next st count (29, 33, 38, 43, 48) sts, PM in this st] 3 times.

You should have 14 (16, 18, 21, 23) sts before the first M, [(28, 32, 37, 42, 47) sts before the next M)] 3 times, 14 (16, 19, 21, 24) sts after the last M.

Row 2: *(Tps, X) to 1 st before M, Tps in st before M, Inc, Tss in M, Inc, rep from * 3 more times, (Tps, X) across, end st. 124 (140, 160, 180, 200) sts

Row 3: *(Tps, X) to 1 st before M, Tss in st before M, do not Inc before or after M, Tss in M, Tss in next st, rep from * 3 more times, (Tps, X) across, end st.

Row 4: *(Tps, X) across placing Tss in st before M, Inc, Tss in M, Inc, Tss in next st, rep from * 3 more times, (Tps, X) across, end st. 132 (148, 168, 188, 208) sts

Row 5: *(Tps, X) placing X before M, do not Inc before or after M, Tss in M, X, rep from * 3 more times, cont in patt across.

Row 6: *Work in patt to M, Inc before M, Tss in M, no Inc after M, cont in patt to next M, no Inc before M, Tss in M, Inc after M, rep from * cont in patt across. 136 (152, 172, 192, 212) sts

Row 7: *Work in patt placing Tps in st before M, Inc before M, Tss in M, no Inc after M, cont in patt to next M, no Inc before next M, Tss in M, Inc after M, Tps in next st, rep from *, cont in patt across. 140 (156, 176, 196, 216) sts

Row 8: *Work in patt placing Tss in st before M, Inc before M, Tss in M, no Inc after M, cont in patt to next M, no Inc before M, Tss in M, Inc after M, Tss in next st, rep from *, cont in patt across. 144 (160, 180, 200, 220) sts

Row 9: *Work in patt to M, no Inc before or after M, X, Tps in M, X, rep from *, cont in patt across. Remove M. From this point on, all sts are in patt.

Row 10: Work even in patt across. All previously marked sts are now Tps.

Work a *total of* 56 (60, 64, 68, 72) rows, or adjust length as desired, keeping in mind this will affect yarn quantities needed for project.

Waistband

I prefer to insert hook under 2 loops when working into the base ch, but in this case, working into the base of X-sts can be difficult, so one loop is fine (2 loops everywhere else).

Join yarn in top right (left for left-handers) corner and draw up loop, draw up loop in each base ch across. 116 (132, 152, 172, 192) sts

Next row: *Tss in next 12 sts, Tss2tog, rep from * across, Tss in each rem st. 108 (123, 142, 160, 179) sts

Next row: Tss in next 4 sts, Tss2tog, *Tss in next 10 sts, Tss2tog, rep from * across, Tss in each rem st, end off. 99 (113, 131, 147, 165) sts

FINISHING
Button Flap

The yarn overs in Row 2 below create a space for the buttonhole. In Row 3, insert hook in the yarn over, which looks like a slanted line wrapped around the return row.

Row 1: Working along side edge, join yarn at top left corner, draw up loop in first row-end and next 18 row-ends. Work Rtn row. 19 sts

Row 2: Tss in next st, yo, sk next st, *Tss in next 6 sts, yo, sk next st, rep from *, yo, sk next st, end st.

Row 3: Tss in each Tss and in each yo across.

Sew seam from just below button flap to 4–5 in./ 10–13 cm above hem.

Sew buttons opposite buttonholes.

Sew half of each snap close to inside edge of right button flap. Try on skirt with closed buttons, mark where 2nd half of snaps should be placed to match first half placement, then sew on.

Block as needed.

This long jacket will keep you cozy and stylish on a chilly day. The body is A-line-shaped to provide comfort and ease whatever you're doing. And yes, there is a pocket! Regina is worked entirely in Tss with a trim of regular crochet.

The venerable Lion Brand Yarn company has been around for over one hundred years. While mostly found at big box stores, it has a separate line, LB Collection, that is available online only. There are some very attractive yarns in this line, and I was thrilled to find this Chainette worsted weight alpaca/nylon blend for this outerwear garment. Chainette is a type of yarn construction that creates yarn of excellent softness and drape and interesting surface texture—a good mix for Tunisian simple stitch.

NOTES

Since this is worked top down beginning at the neckline, the first thing you will encounter is shaping for the front neckline. It involves working increases at the start and end of the second row, to curve the neckline a bit. On the next row, in order for each Front piece to reach its full width, chains are added.

The Front edges of this design overlap to provide an area for buttons and buttonholes. Buttonholes are incorporated into the pattern throughout. They begin in Row 7 and are worked every 6th row thereafter.

This design is worked in Tunisian simple stitch except for the raglan line, which consists of a single Tunisian knit stitch. When making raglan increases, you will notice that the Tks sits a bit lower than the increase stitches on either side of it. Work these Tks sts loosely to counter this tendency. Further, while working increases, spread the stitches out so you can clearly see where to insert your hook. The increase stitch *after* the Tks is particularly tricky: Be sure to insert the hook between the Tks stitch and the back vertical bar of the adjacent stitch.

When beginning the Body, we will draw up a loop in one leg of each raglan stitch, which will add four stitches to the count in Row 1 of Body.

About Body shaping: To provide a roomy fit around the hips, widely spaced increases are worked along the side body. This enlarges the fabric gradually, with a total of about 5 in./13 cm added at the hem. Here we use a different kind of increase than at the neckline—one that is invisible. Keep in mind that in order for the increases to be correctly centered at the side body, we alternate where they are placed: first in M, then in the stitch after M, alternating each time. If you prefer a closer fit throughout the body, omit any Body shaping and work even throughout.

Sleeve shaping: The sleeve is kept quite full down to the elbow, then it narrows rapidly approaching the wrist.

Finishing: While regular crochet is used to finish the neckline, cuffs, and hem, instructions vary a bit in each case. The neckline is meant to tighten more closely around the neck, the sleeve cuffs puff out then pull back in, while the bottom finish should not change the fabric dimension at all but should create a flat edge that does not curl.

FINISHED BUST MEASUREMENTS

Sizes 1 through 5.

40.5 (45, 51, 55.5, 60) in./103 (114.5, 129.5, 141, 152.5) cm

Suggested ease: 4–7 in./10–17.5 cm

MATERIALS

- LB Collection Chainette; 65% baby alpaca, 35% nylon; 115 yds./105 m per 1.75 oz./50g; worsted weight; Mustard #478-159C: 9 (11, 12, 14, 16) balls
- Suggested hook sizes:
  - L-11 (8.0 mm) cabled Tunisian hook
  - J-10 (6.0 mm) regular crochet hook (for trim only)
- 4 stitch markers
- 8 (8, 8, 9, 9) buttons, 1 in./2.5 cm diameter

GAUGE

8 sts and 7 rows = 3 in./7.5 cm

Gauge Swatch

Ch 16.

Work foundation row.

Row 1: Tss across, end st.

Rep Row 1 until you have *a total of* 14 rows.

Regina

SPECIAL STITCHES AND ABBREVIATIONS

Increase (Inc): Draw up loop in space before M, Tks in M, draw up loop in space after M.

Side Increase (SInc): Insert hook in back loop of indicated st and draw up loop. Work next st in front vertical bar of the same st.

Decrease (Dec): At beg of row: Insert hook in next 2 sts, draw up loop. At end of row: Work to last 3 sts, insert hook in next 2 sts, draw up loop, end st.

Buttonhole: Yo, sk next st, Tss in next st. For the following row, draw up a loop in the yo to form a stitch.

Work 2 double crochet together (dc2tog): (Yo, insert hook in designated st, yo and draw up loop, yo and draw through 2 loops) twice, yo, draw through 3 loops. Note this is for Trim only, which is worked in regular crochet.

YOKE

Ch 39 (39, 45, 47, 49).

Row 1: Work Basic Foundation Row.

Place markers: *PM in 2nd st from edge. Beginning in next st count 9 (9, 11, 11, 11) sts, PM in this st. Now starting from end of row, rep from *. Counting sts between M, you should have 1 st on each Front, 8 (8, 10, 10, 10) sts on each Sleeve, and 17 (17, 19, 21, 23) sts on Back + 4 raglan sts.

Row 2: Tss in each st, Inc at each M. Move markers up on this row and every row hereafter until told otherwise. 47 (47, 53, 55, 57) sts.

Row 3: Draw up loop in next ch (neck increase made), Inc at each M, draw up loop in last ch (neck increase made), end st. 57 (57, 63, 65, 67) sts. Fronts: 4 sts; Back: 21 (21, 23, 25, 27) sts; Sleeves:12 (12, 14, 14, 14) sts

With separate strand, join yarn in last st of row, ch 8 (8, 9, 10, 11), end off.

Row 4: Ch 8 (8, 9, 10, 11), draw up loop in each ch just made, Tss across, Inc at each M, draw up loop in each ch, cont in Tss. 169 sts. Fronts: 24 sts; Back: 45 sts; Sleeves: 36 sts

Rows 5 and 6: Inc at each M. 97 (97, 105, 109, 113) sts

Row 7: Work in patt with increases to 4th st from end. Work buttonhole. 105 (105, 113, 117, 121) sts

Row 8: Work in patt with increases, finishing buttonhole. 113 (113, 121, 125, 129) sts

Rows 9–12: Work in patt with increases. 145 (145, 152, 157, 161) sts

Row 13 (Buttonhole row): Rep Row 7. 153 (153, 161, 165, 169) sts

Rows 14–15 (14–16, 14–15, 14–15, 14–15): Work in patt with increases. 169 (177, 177, 181, 185) sts. Fronts: 24 (25, 25, 26, 27) sts; Back: 45 (47, 47, 49, 51) sts; Sleeves: 36 (38, 38, 38, 38) sts

Size 1 Only:

Rows 16 and 17: Tss in each st to M, do not increase at any M, work Tks in each M. Move M up each row. End of Yoke. 169 sts 24, Front 45 back 36 sleeve

From this point on, there will be no further increases in Sleeve, only on Body.

Sizes 2, 3, 4, and 5 Only:

Row(s) 17 (16–19, 16–21, 16–22): Inc before 1st M but not after, no Inc before 2nd M, Inc after 2nd M, Inc before 3rd M but not after, no Inc before 4th M, Inc after 4th M. Sizes 3, 4, and 5, make Buttonhole at end of Row 19. 181 (193, 205, 213) sts. Fronts: 26 (29, 32, 34) sts; Back: 49 (55, 61, 65); Sleeves: 38 (38, 38, 38)

Sizes 2 and 4 Only:

Row 18 (21): Work even with no increases.

You should have 45 (49, 55, 61, 65) sts on Back, 24 (26, 29, 32, 34) sts each Front, 36 (38, 38, 38, 38) sts each Sleeve.

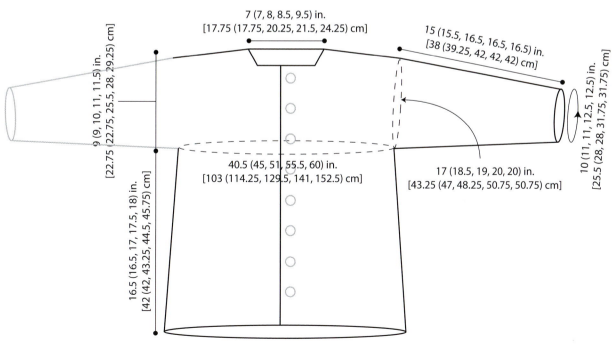

Regina 109

With separate strand, join yarn in first M, ch 7 (9, 11, 13, 13), sl st to 2nd M, end off.

With separate strand, join yarn in 3rd M, ch 7 (9, 11, 13, 13), sl st to 4th M, end off.

BODY

Note: Continue working Buttonhole at end of every 6th row, counting rows from the last Buttonhole on Yoke as starting point. Work a total of 8 (8, 8, 9, 9) Buttonholes, then work Tss to end of row.

Row 1: *Tss in each st to M, Tss in **right leg of M**, draw up loop in each ch, Tss in **left leg of next M**, rep from * across. Remove all M. 4 sts are gained by adding raglan stitches. 111 (123, 139, 155, 163)
Rows 2–4: Work even.

There are an odd number of stitches added at each armhole. Find the center stitch and follow it down to the corresponding stitch in previous row. PM in this stitch on both sides of garment.

Row 5: Make Sinc at each M. 113 (125, 141, 153, 165) sts. Move M down to next row.

Rows 6–9: Work even around.
Row 10: Make SInc in st after M. 115 (127, 143, 155, 167) sts

Continue in patt, working Sinc every 5 rows. Move M down each row. Alternate between working Sinc in M and working it in st after M.

Work *a total of* 37 rows, making increases on Rows 15, 20, 25, 30, and 35, ending with 125 (137, 153, 165, 177) sts. Do not end off.

If you prefer a longer garment, work additional rows; if you get to Row 42, make Sinc.

Hem Trim

With regular crochet hook,

Next row: Ch 2, dc in each vertical bar, turn.
Next row: Ch 1, sl st in each dc, end off.

SLEEVES

To shape the Sleeves, we decrease by 1 st, first at the beginning of a row, then at the end of a row. This happens every 3rd row for most of the sleeve,

then, beginning at Row 25, a decrease is made on every row. A few rows are worked even at the end of the sleeve.

Join yarn in center st of underarm.

Row 1: Draw up loop in each st at underarm and in each st around. 45 (49, 51, 53, 53) sts
Row 2: Work even across.
Row 3: Dec at beg of row. 44 (48, 50, 52, 52) sts
Rows 4 and 5: Work even.
Row 6: Dec at end of row. 43 (47, 49, 51, 51) sts

Continue alternating decreases at beg or end of row, every 3rd row, decreasing on Rows 9, 12, 15, 18, 21, and 24. 37 (41, 43, 45, 45) sts.

Rows 25–34 (25–36, 25–38, 25–36, 25–36): Decrease at beg or end of every row.

Size 2 only:
End off.

Sizes 1, 3, 4, and 5:
Row(s) 35 (37, 37–38, 37–39): Work even. End off. 27 (29, 29, 33, 33) sts.

FINISHING
Sew sleeve seams.

Neck Trim
When working around the neckline, insert the hook into the vertical bars that lie below the top edge. This means the top edge will no longer be visible, since you are working over it. Beginning along the top edge of the front, the first few stitches are in a straight line, then work 1 st into each of the three neckline shaping rows, then continue all around the top of the Sleeve and Back, then down along the neckline shaping rows of the opposite side, finishing with the straight top edge.

With regular crochet hook, join yarn at top right neckline (left for left-handers).

Row 1: Ch 2, *dc2tog in next vertical bar and in each bar to raglan st, dc2tog inserting hook under both bars of raglan st, rep from * around neckline, dc2tog in each bar to last st, dc in last st, turn.
Row 2: Ch 1, sc in each st across, turn.
Row 3: Ch 1, sl st in each st across, end off.

Sleeve Trim
With regular crochet hook, join yarn in first st next to seam.

Next row: Ch 2, dc2tog in each vertical bar around, turn.
Next row: Ch 1, sc in each st around, sl st to starting sc, end off.

Block as needed.

Pocket
With Tunisian hook, ch 16.

Work Tss across for 12 rows, Tsl st across, end off.

You can place the pocket on either side of the body, about 2–3 stitches in from the edge, and at a good height for slipping your hand in. Pin pocket in place and check in mirror before sewing. Use yarn and tapestry needle to sew side edges and bottom of pocket to garment surface.

Gather your softest, most cuddly worsteds for this fun stash-buster sweater! The color concept contrasts neutrals against vivid stripes and allows for maximum flexibility for you to adapt the pattern to your own stash. The striping plan intersperses wider and thinner stripes at regular intervals.

To build my palette I started with leftovers from two projects in this book: Nola and Regina. The earthy gold needed some good color company, and it led me to three other yarns where I had just about a ball: a purple alpaca, a dark teal lambswool, and a maroon alpaca blend. Another ball of variegated pastels contrasted and related well to the other colors. Finally, I made a nice size swatch with all the colors mingled in various ways, and from there was able to create the precise sequence I found most pleasing.

I recommend beginning in a similar manner: Find some soft, wearable worsteds where you have at least two or three balls. From there, explore what complements and contrasts with your basic colors. Remember, you can also combine lighter weight yarns to get some interesting hues. And DO swatch! There's only one way to find out what works, and that is to make a trial run. After making a swatch, I find it helpful to let it sit for several days—by that time I have a good idea of what color combos are most pleasing.

Frida is oversized, and the construction is top down, using shaping that is my own method. My goal was to create a Yoke with regular increases that are not in the usual raglan style. Raglan shaping creates a square neckline and four points at the bottom of the Yoke that determine the stitches for the Body and Sleeve. For a different approach, I increased at six points placed at regular intervals, resulting in a round neckline and a smooth edge at the bottom of the Yoke that allow stitches to be distributed on Body and Sleeves freely. As you move markers up each row, note that every increase row adds two stitches between markers.

Rows start at the center Back. You may use a connecting stitch to join rows as you go, or work flat and sew a seam. The first option creates a "jog" in the stripes, and the 2nd option does not. When counting your stitches at the end of the Yoke, keep in mind that the Back is in two parts, that the total number of stitches on the Back includes both parts, and that this total will match the number of stitches on Front.

FINISHED BUST MEASUREMENTS

Sizes 1 through 5.

39.5 (43.5, 48, 53.5, 57.5) in./100 (110.5, 122, 136, 146) cm

Suggested ease: 5–10 in./13–25.5 cm

MATERIALS

- Approx. 1200 (1400, 1600, 1800, 2000) yds./1098 (1280, 1463, 1646, 1829) m of worsted weight yarn in seven different colors.
- Color Code
    - A: off-white
    - B: gold
    - C: purple
    - D: tan
    - E: teal
    - F: maroon
    - G: variegated pastels
- Suggested hook sizes:
    - K-10½ (6.5 mm) cabled Tunisian hook
    - I-9 (5.5 mm) regular crochet hook (for neckline finishing only)
- 6 stitch markers

GAUGE

12 sts and 14 rows = 4 in./10 cm

Gauge Swatch

Ch 18.

Row 1: Work basic foundation row.
Row 2: Tks across, end st.

Rep Row 2 until you have *a total of* 21 rows.

SPECIAL STITCHES AND ABBREVIATIONS

Inc: Draw up loop in sp before M, Tks in M, draw up loop in sp after M (same as Tfs.)

Decrease at each end: Tks2tog, work in patt to last 3 sts, Tks2tog, end st.

Tks2tog: Insert hook in front bar of next st (as in Tss), then insert hook in following st as in Tks, draw up loop.

Frida

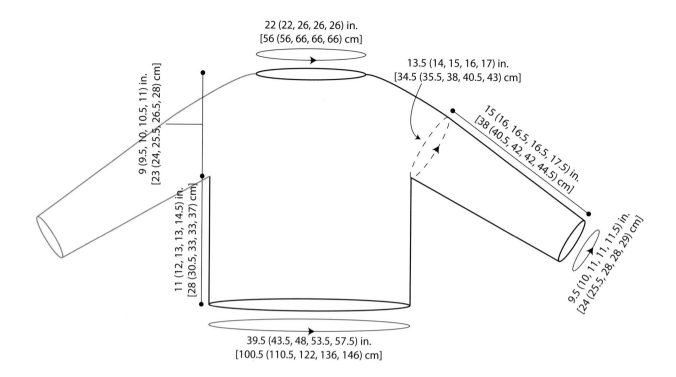

22 (22, 26, 26, 26) in.
[56 (56, 66, 66, 66) cm]

13.5 (14, 15, 16, 17) in.
[34.5 (35.5, 38, 40.5, 43) cm]

9 (9.5, 10, 10.5, 11) in.
[23 (24, 25.5, 26.5, 28) cm]

15 (16, 16.5, 16.5, 17.5) in.
[38 (40.5, 42, 42, 44.5) cm]

11 (12, 13, 13, 14.5) in.
[28 (30.5, 33, 33, 37) cm]

9.5 (10, 11, 11, 11.5) in.
[24 (25.5, 28, 28, 29) cm]

39.5 (43.5, 48, 53.5, 57.5) in.
[100.5 (110.5, 122, 136, 146) cm]

YOKE

Note: The design is worked entirely in Tks.

Follow the instructions below **while at the same time changing colors** as indicated in Stripe Pattern.

Stripe Pattern for Yoke

A: 6 (7, 7, 8, 8) rows
B: 3 (3, 3, 3, 4) rows
C: 3 (3, 3, 3, 4) rows
D: 6 (7, 7, 8, 8) rows
E: 3 (3, 3, 3, 4) rows
B: 3 (3, 3, 3, 4) rows
A: 3 (3, 3, 3, 4) rows

With A, ch 66, (66, 78, 78, 78).

Row 1: Work Basic Foundation Row.

Count 5 (5, 6, 6, 6) sts, PM in next st, *beg in next st count 10 (10, 12, 12, 12) sts, PM in next st, rep from * 4 more times. You should have 6 markers with 10 (10, 10, 12, 12, 12) sts between them, and 5 (5, 6, 6, 6) sts rem after placing last M.

Row 2: Inc at each M. Move M up each row. 78 (78, 90, 90, 90) sts
Row 3: Work even.

From this point, work even and increase on rows as shown below. Each increase row adds 12 sts to your total stitch count.

Size 1:

Increase at each M on rows 5, 8, 11, 14, 17, 20, 23, 26, ending with 174 sts. Work one more row even for a *total of* 27 rows on Yoke.

Size 2:

Increase at each M on rows 4, 7, 10, 13, 16, 19, 22, 25, 28 ending with 186 sts. Work one more row even for a *total of* 29 Rows on Yoke.

Size 3:

Increase at each M on rows 5, 8, 11, 14, 17, 20, 23, 26, 29 ending with 198 sts, 29 Rows total on Yoke.

116 The Tunisian Crochet Sweater Collection

Size 4:
Increase at each M on rows 4, 6, 8, 10, 13, 16, 19, 22, 25, 28, 31 ending with 222 sts, 31 Rows total on yoke.

Size 5:
Inc at each M on rows: 4, 6, 8, 10, 12, 15, 18, 20, 23, 26, 29, 31, 33 ending with 246 sts, 33 Rows total on yoke.

All Sizes:
Remove all M. End off.

BODY

Count 26 (29, 31, 35, 38) sts for half back, PM in this st. Beg in next st count 34 (35, 36, 39, 41) sts for Sleeve, PM in this st. Beg at end of row count 27, (29, 32, 36, 38) sts for half back, PM in this st. Beg in next st count 34 (35, 36, 39, 41) for Sleeve, PM in this st. You have 53 (58, 63, 71, 76) sts each on Front/Back and 34 (35, 36, 39, 41) sts on each Sleeve.

With separate strand, join yarn in first M, *ch 6, (7, 9, 9, 10)** sl st to 2nd M, end off. Join yarn in 3rd M and rep from * to **, sl st to 4th M, end off.

Row 1: Join color A in first M and work even, drawing up loop in each ch at the underarms.

Stripe Pattern for Body
A: 5 (6, 7, 7, 7) rows
F: 3 (3, 3, 3, 4) rows
B: 3 (3, 3, 3, 4) rows
G: 8 (9, 10, 10, 10) rows
B: 3 (3, 3, 3, 4) rows
E: 3 (3, 3, 3, 4) rows
D: 8 (9, 10, 10, 10) rows
F: 3 (3, 3, 3, 4) rows
B: 3 (3, 3, 3, 4) rows

You should have *a total of* 40 (43, 46, 46, 52) rows. Remove M.

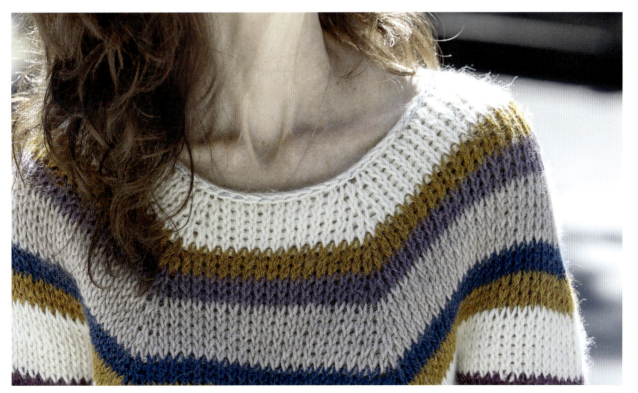

Frida

SLEEVES

Join color A in center st of underarm, draw up loop in this st and each underarm st, Tks in each st around sleeve, draw up loop in rem sts of underarm. 40 (42, 45, 48, 51) sts

Following Stripe Pattern for Body, work 14 (17, 20, 20, 26) rows even.

Next row: Dec 1 st at each end.
Next 3 rows: Work even.

Rep last 4 rows 5 (5, 6, 7, 7) times, ending with 28 (30, 31, 32, 35) sts

Now continue with this stripe pattern, working even:

G: 8 (9, 6, 2, 2) rows
B: 3 (3, 3, 3, 0) rows
E: 3 (3, 0, 0, 0) rows.

Tss sl st across, end off.

FINISHING

To keep neckline from stretching over time (due to the weight of the garment), I recommend a slip stitch finish worked with two worsted weight yarns held together. I used A and E. If this appears too thick, you can try it with just one strand.

With regular crochet hook, join yarn at center back neck at "seam," sl st tightly all around neckline, end off.

Block as needed. Sew sleeve seam.

Zoey

Fluffy yarn makes Zoey a fun, oversized pullover. The stitches used are Tss and Tunisian Puffs, which are very similar to puffs in regular crochet. It is worked top down but instead of increasing at raglan points, we add stitches on rows where it's easy to do, the rows made entirely with Tss. The result is a rounded neckline instead of the rectangle that raglan shaping produces.

Zoey will work over a wide range of bodies. Because the yarn is so light, it can have anywhere from 3–12 in./7.5–30.5 cm of ease over bust circumference. The length extends to the waist or a little below and, like all top-down sweaters, can easily be adjusted.

Laines du Nord is an Italian yarn company offering rather luxurious fibers. Cashsilk features merino, cashmere, and silk, and I just couldn't resist! Or use a similarly fluffy yarn, possibly with mohair or angora, classified as a sport weight yarn. Keep in mind the design is worked with a large hook: size L-11 (8 mm). For this reason, a yarn with no fuzz will yield a very different effect.

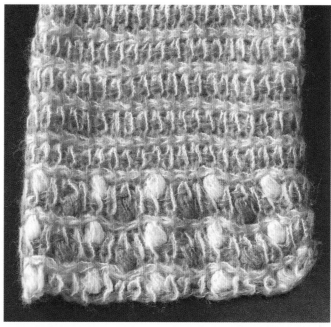

Bottom of sleeve

STITCH PATTERN

The pattern consists of Tunisian simple stitches interspersed with Puff stitches. A few rows on the Yoke are worked in Tss only, and the Sleeves use Tss except for the bottom rows. The Puffs always have 3 Tss between them and are staggered in alternating rows. The puffs in the next row will be worked into the center stitch of those 3 Tss.

Tunisian Puff stitch in progress

When making Puff stitches, two things can go wrong in the process of drawing through all the loops on the hook: Either you inadvertently include the adjacent stitch just before the puff, which means you will lose a stitch, or, conversely, miss a yarn over when drawing through, which means you may find yourself with an extra stitch. If you don't catch the error when it's made, you can compensate on the next row, either by drawing up a loop in the missed stitch, or by not drawing up a loop in the added stitch.

NOTES ON CHANGING COLORS

In this design every row uses two colors, and the color change always occurs on the return row: You will pick up stitches with one color and use the second color for the return. Then continue with the second color for the following forward row, and change back to the first color on the return row. Because we are making this color change, the last stitch in the forward row can become loose. Two things will help: As you draw up the alternate color from two rows below, bring yarn from back to front crossing over the current color, and be careful to regulate tension so that the end stitch is not too loose or tight.

MATERIALS

- Laines du Nord Cashsilk Light; 68% merino, 22% silk, 10% cashmere; 158 yds./144.5 m per 0.9 oz./25 g; sport weight; 5 (6, 8) balls each of Teal Green #3041 (A) and Seafoam #3042 (B)
- Suggested hook sizes:
  - L-11 (8.0 mm) cabled Tunisian hook
  - I-9 (5.5 mm) regular crochet hook (for finishing only)
- 16 stitch markers

FINISHED BUST MEASUREMENTS

Sizes 1 (S/M), 2 (L/1X), and 3 (2X).

47.5 (55, 61) in./120.5 (139.5, 155) cm

GAUGE

6 Tss and 5 rows = 2 in./5 cm

Puff Patt: 8 sts and 5 rows = 3 in./7.5 cm

Gauge Swatch

Ch 19.

Work foundation row.

Row 1: 2 Tss, *Puff, 3 Tss, rep from * across, ending with 2 Tss, end st.

Row 2: *Puff, 3 Tss, rep from * across, ending with Puff, end st.

Rep Rows 1 and 2 until you have *a total of* 10 rows.

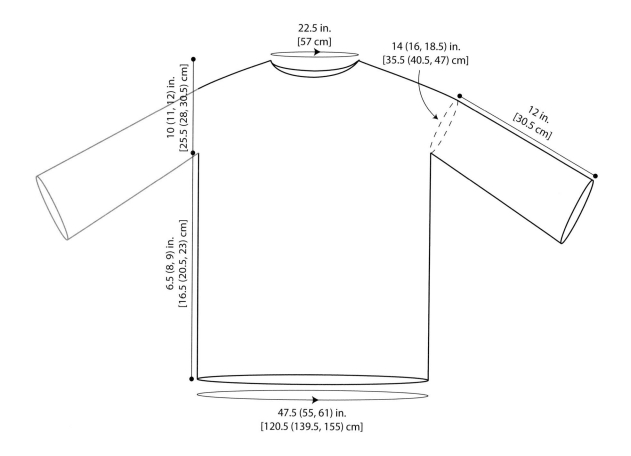

SPECIAL STITCHES AND ABBREVIATIONS

Puff: (Yo, insert hook in next vertical bar and draw up loop) 3 times, yo, draw through 6 loops.

Increase (Inc): Draw up loop in sp before M (as in Tfs), Tss in M, draw up loop in sp after M. This adds 2 sts at each increase point.

YOKE

With A, ch 67.

Row 1 Fwd: Draw up loop in each ch. **Rtn:** Change to B, work regular Rtn row here and throughout.
Row 2: 2 Tss, *Puff, 3 Tss, rep from * across, ending with 2 Tss, end st. **Rtn:** Change to A.
Row 3: *Puff, 3 Tss, rep from * across, ending with Puff, end st. **Rtn:** Change to B.

PM in 4th st, *beg in next st count 4 sts, PM in this st, rep from * across. 16M placed.

Yoke Shaping

Row 4: 2 Tss, *Inc, 3 Tss, rep from * across, ending with 2 Tss, end st. **Rtn:** Change to A. 99 sts

Move M up to center st of Inc.

Row 5: Tss in each st working Inc at each M. **Rtn:** Change to B. 131 sts
Row 6: Rep Row 3. **Rtn:** Change to A.
Row 7: Rep Row 2. **Rtn:** Change to B.
Rows 8 and 9: Rep last 2 rows.

For the rest of this patt, cont changing colors every Rtn row.

Row 10: Work even in Tss.
Row 11: 2 Tss, *Inc, 7 Tss, rep from * across, 2 Tss, end st. 163 sts
Row 12: Work even.
Row 13: 2 Tss, *Inc, 9 Tss, rep from * across, 2 Tss, end st. 195 sts
Row 14: Work even.

Size 2 Only:
Row 15: 2 Tss *Inc, 23 Tss, rep from * across, 2 Tss, end st. 211 sts
Row 16: Work even.

Size 3 Only:
Row 15: 2 Tss, *Inc, 11 Tss, rep from * across, 2 Tss, end st. 227 sts
Row 16: Work even.

All Sizes:
Row 15 (17, 17): 3 Tss, *Puff, 3 Tss, rep from * across ending 2 Tss, end st.
Row 16 (18, 18): 5 Tss, *Puff, 3 Tss, rep from * across ending 2 Tss, end st.

Sizes 1 and 2 Only:
Place working loop on holder, cont to Body.

Size 3 Only:
Rows 19 and 20: Rep last 2 rows, cont to Body.

Remove all M. End of Yoke.

*Count 30 (32, 35) sts, PM in this st. Beg in next st count 38 (40, 44) sts, PM in next st. Now starting at end of row, rep from *. You have 30 (32, 35) sts on each half Back, 38 (40, 50) sts on each Sleeve, and 59 (67, 69) sts on Front.

BODY

For all following rows, change color every row on Rtn row as before.

With separate strand, join A in first M, ch 4 (8, 12), sl st to 2nd M, end off. With separate strand, join A in 3rd M, ch 4 (8, 12), sl st to 4th M, end off. Note: When joining yarn for Sleeves, we will join in the 3rd (5th, 7th) ch. Since you will work into this ch for the Body, it's awkward to mark, but you will be able to identify it visually.

Row 1: Pick up working loop, *work in Puff patt to added ch, draw up loop in each ch, rep from *, cont in patt across. Note that these Puffs should line up with the previous row in same color. 127 (147, 163) sts

Rows 2–11 (2–13, 2–15): Cont in Puff patt, end off. Feel free to work more or fewer rows depending on desired length. No sl sts are needed to finish this stitch pattern.

SLEEVE

With A, join yarn in 3rd (5th, 7th) st at underarm.

Work Tss across completing *a total of* 23 rows. Try on here to determine if sleeve should be longer. This is 3 in./7.5 cm from bottom of sleeve. Add any needed rows here before working rem rows.

Next 4 rows: Rep rows 2 and 3 of Body twice.
Next row: Rep row 2. End off.

FINISHING

Block as needed.

Seam Back and Sleeves.

Because this is a very open, lacy fabric, I handled the Back seam a bit differently to avoid large gaps. Instead of matching one row-end to the next, I worked 2 seam stitches in each row-end. Keep in mind that it can be a challenge to match the two sides exactly as the fabric is so flexible and the edge stitches are in different colors. See photo at bottom left for how I pinned the two sides together.

Zoey

Leave long tails at each end for making the top and bottom of seam neat and secure. With RS facing, work back and forth from one side of the seam to the other. Use any available strands near edge. Work needle through one strand at top of seam, then cross to opposite side and work needle through one strand; *remaining on same side, work into next strand, cross over to opposite side, bring needle under next strand. Rep from * to end of seam. At both edges of seam you can work 2 or 3 times into the same spot to secure, but don't allow yarn to become clumpy.

Sleeves use a solid stitch, so the seam can be done in the usual way.

Neckline Finishing

With regular crochet hook, work a round of slip stitches all around neckline to tighten and strengthen. Given the fuzzy yarn, I worked around the entire stitch rather than into the top of the stitch.

Finished seam

Acknowledgments

My thanks to these yarn companies for contributing their beautiful yarns for these projects. I encourage readers to browse the impressive collections of these reputable yarn manufacturers.

Berroco.com	**Lainesdunord.it**
Cascadeyarns.com	**Lionbrand.com**
Hobbii.com	**Malabrigoyarn.com**
JodyLongyarn.com	**Skacelknitting.com**
Knitpicks.com	**Universalyarn.com**
Knittingfever.com	**Urthyarns.com**

I am very grateful for the contribution of photographer Scott Jones, whose sensitivity to light, color, and how textiles work on women's bodies helps showcase each garment so well. Thanks, too, to my gorgeous models: Stacy Fields, Susan Sterman-Jones, and Ruby Jones (Scott's wife, and his daughter!). It was a privilege to work with all of you, and you did more than justice to the garments.

Thank you to my good friend Leslie Johnson, who saw these designs in the making and kept me on track with her feedback and unerring eye.

About the Author

Dora Ohrenstein is a leading crochet designer, author, and teacher. Her chic and innovative designs appear regularly in print and online magazines. She has taught at national events and in yarn shops around the country. Dora is an avid student of crochet history and has published numerous articles on the topic. Find Dora at her website, DoraOhrenstein.com, and on Facebook and Instagram. Dora was a well-known soprano and has taught singing at the college level for many decades.